Lessons from our Students

Meditations on Performance Pedagogy

Stacey Cabaj and
Andrea Odinov

NEW YORK AND LONDON

Designed cover image: © alphaspirit.it/Shutterstock.com

First published 2024
by Routledge
605 Third Avenue, New York, NY 10158

and by Routledge
4 Park Square, Milton Park, Abingdon, Oxon, OX14 4RN

Routledge is an imprint of the Taylor & Francis Group, an informa business

© 2024 Stacey Cabaj and Andrea Odinov

The right of Stacey Cabaj and Andrea Odinov to be identified as authors of this work has been asserted in accordance with sections 77 and 78 of the Copyright, Designs and Patents Act 1988.

All rights reserved. No part of this book may be reprinted or reproduced or utilised in any form or by any electronic, mechanical, or other means, now known or hereafter invented, including photocopying and recording, or in any information storage or retrieval system, without permission in writing from the publishers.

Trademark notice: Product or corporate names may be trademarks or registered trademarks, and are used only for identification and explanation without intent to infringe.

Library of Congress Cataloging-in-Publication Data
Names: Cabaj, Stacey, author. | Odinov, Andrea, author.
Title: Lessons from our students : meditations on performance pedagogy / Stacey Cabaj and Andrea Odinov.
Description: New York, NY : Routledge, 2024. | Includes bibliographical references and index.
Identifiers: LCCN 2023032317 (print) | LCCN 2023032318 (ebook) | ISBN 9780367711580 (hardback) | ISBN 9780367711559 (paperback) | ISBN 9781003149576 (ebook)
Subjects: LCSH: Acting--Study and teaching--Case studies. | Performing arts--Study and teaching--Case studies.
Classification: LCC PN2075 .C24 2024 (print) | LCC PN2075 (ebook) | DDC 792.02/8--dc23/eng/20231010
LC record available at https://lccn.loc.gov/2023032317
LC ebook record available at https://lccn.loc.gov/2023032318

ISBN: 978-0-367-71158-0 (hbk)
ISBN: 978-0-367-71155-9 (pbk)
ISBN: 978-1-003-14957-6 (ebk)

DOI: 10.4324/9781003149576

Typeset in Stempel Garamond
by KnowledgeWorks Global Ltd.

Lessons from our Students

Lessons from our Students: Meditations on Performance Pedagogy is a collection of thirty short personal case studies about pedagogical issues that arise in theater classrooms and rehearsals.

Teaching in the acting and performance classroom is rapidly changing in the early 2020s. In the wake of the global pandemic, online education, massive trauma, and a social justice revolution, educators are seeking wisdom, clarity, and reassurance about their pedagogy. The authors speak to the current moment and the unique challenges of teaching theater by presenting a personal, practical, and authentic expression of vulnerability, humanity, and artistry as teachers. Through thirty personal meditations, the authors pose reflective questions and discussion prompts that evaluate the craft of teaching theater, issues that arise, and ideas about how to respond with vision and integrity. Accompanying exercises invite readers to reflect on their own teaching practices.

This book serves as a text for theater teachers and teachers-in-training in search of inspiration, validation, and transformation in drama education and theater pedagogy classes.

Stacey Cabaj is an Assistant Professor of Acting and Pedagogy at Loyola Marymount University. Her spirited approach to performance is grounded in her teaching certifications in Meditation, the Meisner Technique, Vibrant Voice Technique, Hatha and Vocal Yoga.

Andrea Odinov is a Voice, Speech, and Dialect Specialist, and Clinical Assistant Professor of Voice and Speech at Loyola Marymount University. She has provided coaching for theater companies and actors in the greater Los Angeles area and is a Certified Associate Instructor of Fitzmaurice Voicework®. www.andreaodinov.com

Contents

Acknowledgments viii
Dear Reader ix

Part I
Inhalation 1

1 Why Theater? 3

2 An Ecosystem of Love 5

3 I Am, I Feel, I Am Bringing 7

4 Teacher Talking Time 9

5 The Jargon Finger 11

6 Everything but the Kitchen Sink 13

7 Standard Operating Procedures 16

8 Perennial Questions 19

9 To Grade or to Ungrade 20

10 Evaluations and Evolutions 26

Part II
Exhalation 29

11	Prototypes	31
12	The Wisecracker	33
13	Breakdownthrough	35
14	Permission Slips	38
15	The Psychology of Apology	40
16	Ahimsa	42
17	Whole Body Yes	45
18	Hover and Hunker	48
19	Spoons	51
20	I Need a Champion	53

Part III
Transformation 57

21	Whose Need Is It Anyway?	59
22	Lessons from my Dream Students	65
23	Teaching through Chaos	70
24	When the Teacher Is Not Alright	77

25	Unspeakable Wounds	83
26	There's Always One	97
27	There's More than Meets the Ear	104
28	Lessons from My Recent Role as a Student	109
29	When Death Comes	113
30	Holding Space	115
	Lessons from My Co-Author	*116*
	Bibliography	*119*
	Index	*124*

Acknowledgments

The authors would like to recognize the valuable support and mentorship provided by Dean Bryant Alexander and our colleagues in the Department of Theatre Arts & Dance at Loyola Marymount University.

We are grateful to our team at Routledge for seeing us, hearing our vision, and helping us bring this book into being.

To our loved ones, who have walked alongside us through many hard things, we cherish you.

We offer profound thanks to our teachers for their encouragement, guidance, and wisdom.

And to our students, thank you for sharing your art and your hearts.

Dear Reader

Let's inhale deeply. And exhale completely.

As teachers of theater performance, we often begin our classes with invitations to breathe, center, and open to the present moment… Especially when we're about to do hard things.

In this book, we share stories of chaos, confusion, and follies from our classrooms and rehearsal halls, and how these experiences have transformed our teaching. May our radical openness provide solace and inspiration to you, wherever you are on your teaching journey.

As Catherine Fitzmaurice, the founder of Fitzmaurice Voicework®, has said:

> *"Your students will always be your greatest teachers."*

So, in classes, office hours, and rehearsals, we apprentice ourselves to our students' wisdom. What follows is a collection of some of their lessons, a journey that will unfold in three movements: Inhalation, Exhalation, Transformation.

Inhalation: By breathing in, we are inspired.
Here you'll find ten formative lessons about: content essentialism, purpose and ritual, questioning power structures, (un)grading, and evaluations.

Exhalation: Through breathing out, we are expressed.
Here you'll find ten illustrative stories about our humanity in the classroom, including: embodiment and consent, digital learning, failure, fear, and self-actualization.

Transformation: In holding space, we are transformed.
Here you'll find ten threshold moments where we explore: equity and empowerment, trauma, trust, and transformation.

The book is meant to be a hopeful, helpful, and healing peek into our teaching journals. First up are a few quick tips for our journey:

- There are 30 lessons followed by reflective questions and/or meditative practices. If you're reading this with others (e.g., in a drama education or theater pedagogy class), you might focus on one or two lessons each week of a semester.
- We use the word *meditation* to describe the act of contemplation or reflection through which wisdom may arise. The meditative questions and practices we offer are ones that you might sit with, journal about, or discuss in a class or with a colleague.
- Throughout the book, you'll find images of trees, mountains, walking paths, and water. For us, these are visual metaphors as well as invitations to pause and process.

- To honor the privacy of our students, most lessons do not include identifying information. Where necessary, we use signifying pseudonyms and pronouns.
- We have intentionally created a thin book with thick pages and lots of open space. Please write in it, doodle in it, and make it yours. We'd love to hear about your teaching transformations! @lessonsfromourstudents #lessonsfromourstudents

Shall we begin? You may wish to bring a pen or pencil, some tea, and find a cozy place to be.

May this be of benefit,

Stacey and Andrea
Summer 2023

Labyrinth (Credit: Andrea Odinov)

Part I
Inhalation

Chapter 1
Why Theater?

During graduate school, I had my first interview for a faculty position. A small college, on an island off the coast of Maine, was hiring its *first* professor of theater. I desperately hoped it would be me.

It was a winter campus visit, and I arrived swathed in wool and fleece, but it wasn't the cold that tested me the most. It was a question during a pizza dinner with the student leadership. A small voice from the back of the room called out:

> *But why theater?*

It sounded like a dare. I could feel my heart and mind racing with ideas about how to respond. It was an excellent question and a perennial one. I'd heard it answered in a myriad of ways: by Patsy Rodenburg in her powerful talk "Why I Do Theatre," through Kathleen Gallagher's *Why Theatre Matters: Urban Youth, Engagement, and a Pedagogy of the Real*, and in the collection *Why the Theatre: In Personal Essays, College Teachers, Actors, Directors, and Playwrights Tell Why the Theatre Is So Vital to Them*. But, as an acting teacher, I understood that it was important to experience and respond to the question as if for the first time.

Dear Reader, how would you respond? Would you:

A) Tell a story of theater's transformative power in your life.
B) List the many creative, social, and interpersonal skills that theater cultivates.
C) Describe the possible ways to meaningfully engage the campus and community through theater practice.
D) Invite the student to expand on their curiosity.
E) Other.

In truth, I don't remember exactly how I answered that day. I remember only the student's concern and curiosity, their need for meaning and relevancy in the whole endeavor. And so, years later, before each course I teach and each production I coach, I continue to start with why.

Questions for Meditation:
1. Why do you think theater is important?
2. What would you say to a prospective student (or a non-major) about the value of theater practice?
3. What might you say to a parent/guardian who doesn't want their child to study/major in theater?
4. On your toughest teaching days, what motivates you to return to the classroom?

Chapter 2
An Ecosystem of Love

On the first day of class, we create a community agreement. As the facilitator, I invite each student to consider:

What do you hope to know?
How do you wish to grow?
What is your ideal learning environment?

I ask the students to discuss in pairs:

How shall we dedicate our time together?
How shall we engage with our space?
How shall we mindfully use our technology?

I then gather the full group to exchange ideas about their vision and values. Below are some of their true, beautiful ideals:

We learn best in an ecosystem of love, not an egosystem of fear.
Education is our practice of freedom.
Everybody belongs in our circle; we hold space for everyone's point of view.

We all want to be seen, heard, and able to express our unique authentic selves.

Curiosity and enthusiasm will be our North Stars.

Lifelines feel better than deadlines.

We will be intentional with our attention and kind in our communication.

We will honor each other's time and value each other's presence.

We will prioritize safety, care, and dignity in our space.

We will hold space for each other's development and celebrate each other's discoveries!

Questions for Meditation:

1. What ideals are centered in your classrooms and creative spaces?
2. When you bring these ideals to mind, how do they feel in your body?
3. How does your classroom community navigate disagreement?

Chapter 3
I Am, I Feel, I Am Bringing

Early each semester, I invite the students to share their favorite warm-ups, theater games, and check-ins. Recently, a student brought in a Circle Up Mashup, and this favorite check-in exercise soon became an important part of our class's routine.

Standing or sitting in a circle, each person speaks their truth of the moment:

I am…	(name, pronouns, aspects of identity)
I feel…	(a moment of interoception[1])
I am bringing…	(news, questions, needs, snacks, etc.)
Grounded	(move arms out to the sides)
And Checked	(hands meet overhead)
In.	(hands move downward to heart center.)

There are several reasons why it's a wonderful opening practice:

- it centers the students' knowing, being, and trusting themselves,
- it invites their whole personhood into the classroom community space,
- it engages students' bodies through breath and movement, inviting more present-moment awareness,

- it's an opportunity to hear/feel the students' voices/energies and recalibrate the lesson plan to their needs,
- it provides students an opportunity to practice their communication skills and build community.

Questions for Meditation:

1. What is a class check-in routine or ritual that you find useful?
2. What is a class check-out or closure practice that you value?
3. How do you calibrate your lesson plan to your students' energy and needs?

Note

1 Awareness of internal sensations.

Chapter 4
Teacher Talking Time

Student: I can always tell if I'm going to like a class by how much TTT there is on the first day.

Me: ...TTT?

Student: Teacher Talking Time. The more TTT in a course, the less enjoyable and engaging it's going to be for me.

While my graduate teacher training covered the concepts of teacher-centered, student-centered, and subject-centered classrooms, the notion of TTT was a revelation to me. It originated in the Communicative Language Teaching framework, which highlighted the value of Student Talking Time (STT) in foreign language acquisition. As my brilliant student suggests, this also applies to drama and theater classes.

In a teacher-centered classroom with high TTT, the teacher determines what content is introduced and when. However, this often correlates with limited skill practice and autonomy for learners, which can lead to decreased concentration and increased boredom.

Conversely, creating more opportunities for STT can facilitate greater engagement, idea generation, and focus.

An essential lesson for teachers is that *talking at* learners is not often conducive to their learning.

So, how do we reduce unnecessary TTT?

As a shorthand, one can begin to practice by asking oneself the question:

W.A.I.T.
Why Am I Talking?

If you're not sure, you can give yourself a Teacher Talking Time-Out. You can then diversify your instruction (vary your teaching tactics) by inviting questions or reflections, facilitating a Think-Pair-Share, or holding space for silence.

Questions for Meditation:
1. What is the typical ratio of TTT to STT in your classroom?
2. How long are your demonstrations or lectures?
3. Do you leave space/silence for learners to work without your verbal input?
4. Do you feel guilty or uncomfortable when you're not giving verbal feedback?

Chapter 5
The Jargon Finger

She confessed: "I often feel dumb in our class. Everyone else uses these fancy words and I don't know what they mean...I feel behind and like I don't belong here."

My heart ached for this first-generation student. The world had given her a memo that bigger words = smarter, smarter = better, and better = belonging. I had also gotten that cultural memo and had spent much of my life climbing the academic ladder and its rungs of elitist jargon. We had both experienced Jargon-Monoxide Poisoning, a term coined by Kathy Klotz-Guest to stress that jargon pollutes one's message and dilutes its clarity.

So, the student and I decided to implement The Jargon Finger in our next class. Whenever a word is used in class with a confusing meaning, someone raises and wiggles their index finger in the air. This subtle sign is a call-in for the speaker to explain and unpack the word, and this contributes to the democratization[1] of knowledge in the classroom.

Language has the power
to be a bridge
or
to be a barrier
to understanding.

Question for Meditation:
1. What does it feel like to say the words "I don't know"?
2. What cultural memos have you inherited about intelligence, language, and power?
3. What kind of community agreements or norms might you create with your students to address barriers to understanding?
4. Music Meditation: Listen to Weird Al Yankovic's song "Mission Statement," which satirizes corporate jargon. What terms might be considered theater jargon? Academic jargon?

Note
1   Democratize: to make something accessible to everyone.

Chapter 6
Everything but the Kitchen Sink

It was November, or what felt more like the 687th of March during the Pandemic of 2020. Students were tired. I was also tired. Seemingly endless hours of screen time were taking their toll. I had planned an assignment precisely for this point in the semester, which was a check-in. I wanted to know how they were doing, and how their understanding and integration of the coursework were faring.

I feel like I am learning so much without being overwhelmed, and I appreciate that greatly, a student wrote, before expressing feelings of stress and fatigue from other courses.

Those words released the hold on my breath, and on that breath rode a sigh of empathy.

I'm no stranger to overwhelm. When we, as educators, moved our entire pedagogies online, I experienced a whole new dynamic of anxiety. Course modules seemed like empty closets to be filled with as many videos, articles, assignments, and resources the technology could hold. The self-imposed pressure to build the shiniest, most engaging, and yet, rigorous online course was palpable. It felt like overpacking for a trip to an unfamiliar destination. While sorting through an abundance of online learning tool options, I had to ask myself the same question I ask when online shopping: *Do I really need this?* And, more specifically, *Do I really need this, now?*

This "now" is unlike anything we've experienced before: sequestered, perhaps solitary, and separated from both normal academic life and life in general. But even if "now" were what it once was, I'm considering what is essential for my students, and what is essential for me.

Optimally, teachers never stop learning, and the desire to empower our students with decades of knowledge and expertise can feel like an educational bombardment. Loading course modules and syllabi with resources and assignments that we might not expect them to read or do but offer with a gentle and well-intended "They're just there for you," can create anxiety and even resentment for what they feel is "busy work," especially when multiplied by the work in their other courses.

A familiar rabbit hole opens: Do they need this information, or do I need to give it to them? Am I trying to sell them on how important (and vast) this subject is and how much I know about it? What is truly essential to achieve the course's learning outcomes and inspire continued learning? Can I trust them to tell me if they're hungry for more or if they're full? Do they feel they can tell me? Where is their overwhelm threshold? Is it a moving marker? Deep breaths...

My class is not their only class, nor their only responsibility, nor their only area of interest (if it even is). I certainly want them engaging with material outside of class. I want them to embody what they're learning, be intellectually stimulated and challenged by it, educated, and continually curious. I sincerely hope that if I am mindful—listening to them and to me, then we'll both know if there's room, or need, for the kitchen sink.

(Just one) Question:
What do you feel is essential in your course?

Chapter 7
Standard Operating Procedures

It was midterms. Each student in our voice class had selected and rehearsed a poem through which to practice their technique. The class decided to convene in the campus' amphitheater, with its green expanse and magnificent view of the sunset.

As the students began vocal warmups, two uniformed Reserve Officers' Training Core (ROTC) cadets started unpacking their gear stage left. I saw my students look around, cautiously, and I approached the cadets to inquire about their plans for the next hour.

"It should work out; the platoon meets here at 4:30."

At 4:25, the last student took the stage to share the poem that he had memorized: "Insensibility" by Wilfred Owen. He stood downstage facing his peers, who were seated in a semicircle. Behind him, the sun had begun to set. He spoke softly, with conviction:

> Happy are men who yet before they are killed
>
> Can let their veins run cold.

At 4:26, the calls began in the distance: "ABOUT FACE. RIGHT SHOULDER ARMS. FORWARD MARCH."

He trembled and steadied himself. I wondered if I should intercede.

> And some cease feeling
>
> Even themselves or for themselves.
>
> Dullness best solves
>
> The tease and doubt of shelling…

Dozens of young cadets marched into view as the platoon leader bellowed: "LEFT FLANK MARCH, RIGHT FLANK MARCH."

My students looked nervously at each other, wondering if we should clear the space.

I looked at my watch. 4:28. With steely resolve, the student continued:

> Happy are these who lose imagination:
>
> They have enough to carry with ammunition.

The platoon stood in formation as the officer called: "PRESENT ARMS."

4:29. The officers, the platoon, the students, and I waited for the next directive.

The poet's words cut through the tense silence.

> By choice they made themselves immune
> To pity and whatever mourns in man
> Before the last sea and the hapless stars;
> Whatever mourns when many leave these shores;

Whatever shares
The eternal reciprocity of tears.

We exhaled, applauded, and retreated from the amphitheater to debrief on the midterm experience. I was in awe of all the students' progress, but especially of the brave young heart who spoke his poem with such determination. How did he maintain his composure in the presence and pressure of advancing troops? It was simple, he said:

> *As an artist,*
> *my Standard Operating Procedure*
> *is to stay grounded*
> *and speak the truth.*

Questions for Meditation:
1. How do you know when to end a class exercise? How do you signal this to students?
2. What are the Standard Operating Procedures at your school or institution about space, time, and communication?
3. What are the Standard Operating Procedures in your classroom: to speak in discussion, to leave the room, to submit assignments, etcetera?
4. How do you establish these? Through directives or consensus?

Chapter 8
Perennial Questions

Some classroom questions have clear, simple, and easy answers. Others benefit from a pause for discernment.

Imagine that you are teaching a class and your students ask you some of these perennial questions. Pause and notice what thoughts/feelings arise. Consider your possible reply and the factors in your decision-making:

1. Is attendance mandatory?
2. How do I get an A in your class?
3. Can the class have your phone number?
4. How long does [the assignment] have to be?
5. Can I talk about God here?
6. What's the right answer?
7. Do I have what it takes to make it?
8. Will you come and see our show?
9. Did you like it? Was it good? Was I good?
10. What's wrong with me?

Chapter 9
To Grade or to Ungrade

I would rather sleep on a bag of books than grade performance-based classes, but in an academic institution, that's part of the job. A grade must be submitted for each of my very individual students with very individual levels of experience, skill, and that absurdly subjective and loaded word—talent. To do so, I needed an assessment process that avoided subjectivity, and I consulted with colleagues who generously shared their grading structures, feeling that this would ensure a structure that was both university—and student—approved. It looked something like this:

Attendance, Participation, and Progress	[insert point value]
Quizzes or Written Assignments	[insert point value]
Midterm	[insert point value]
Final	[insert point value]

Students seemed to accept this format as routinely as I created it. We were all used to historical grading language such as "getting a grade" and "giving a grade," no matter how much I reinforced that grades are earned, not given. But, in truth, wasn't I doing the giving here? I was dictating a point value to assess their education. I never liked it—sitting with a calculator at the end of the semester, feeling sick about why 83 points was a B-, but 84 points was a B, and wishing they had only been absent twice instead of three times...but I did it. No one challenged their grade, and I didn't challenge my methods. Wash, rinse, repeat...until I taught online, during the 2020 pandemic.

Everything had to change—lifestyle and learning. How could I assign a point value to attendance, when some of my students were in radically different time zones, or their Wi-Fi connection was so unstable that even if they could log into class, they would be disconnected within minutes? Participation points seemed to lose their value, as students, in general, became more reticent within their rectangles, especially if their home environment was chaotic. I had to rethink course objectives, content, and ultimately, assessment, not to "dumb things down" or make an "A" easy to achieve (as academic critics who never worked a day in academia might say), but to make education more meaningful and effective. Performance classes are not as easily quantifiable as subjects such as math, where one either solves the problem or one doesn't.

Enter "ungrading": a student-centered self-assessment model that abandons a dictated point system and encourages student agency, engaged learning, and self-evaluation. I was wary of it at first. What if students put in minimal effort and, in some delusion of grandeur, give themselves all As? How would I have the hard conversations about grade discrepancies? Did I trust them to assess themselves?

In speaking with colleagues who were also experimenting with ungrading and yielding positive outcomes, I decided to try it out, using the following language:

> Your self-reflection and evaluation give you more agency over your learning process. It's an opportunity for your own standards, your own reflection, and your own educational journey. You won't have to wonder where you stand with your grade, or why 83 points is a different letter grade than 84. If you can evaluate your own work, then the value of your work can't be dictated by others.

If, according to the university, an A = Superior, B = Good, C = Satisfactory, D = Poor, and F = Failure, then what constitutes their superior, or highest quality work in terms of attendance, participation, engagement, and written work…? How would their highest quality of work differ from work that is "good" or "satisfactory"? Does "highest quality" = perfect? What did those letters and their descriptions mean to them? The syllabus outlined the available instructional methods and learning materials, and noted that I would be tracking their work, offering feedback when appropriate. In turn, they were asked to track their work too, holding themselves accountable to the standards they set for the desired letter grade. At the semester's end, they were to submit a process letter: a detailed reflection and self-assessment of their experience with the course's learning outcomes and how their work achieved those learning outcomes. I asked for conscious introspection and gentle honesty in these assessments. During Finals Week, I met with each student individually to discuss their process letters, and together we assigned a university letter grade to their coursework. Some students felt comfortable assigning themselves a grade in their process letter prior to our meeting, in which case I would offer a response to their assessment.

If I may be frank, ungrading was much more work than unconscious grading. I found myself giving more individualized feedback following assignments, and students requested more office-hour appointments. The final week of the semester (when everyone is running on fumes) was filled with reading pages of process letters and individual meetings for discussion.

I learned that I loved it. These process conversations offered me an opportunity to know my students even more and to discuss subsequent steps for study. The letters and conversations were informative, enlightening, and very helpful to me in guiding future instruction. Some students appreciated it and found it freeing, and for others, it triggered anxiety. For those who experienced self-evaluation stress, we leaned into that discomfort and reflected upon why that discomfort existed. I empathized with them and shared that writing my annual faculty self-assessment report brought up the same feelings for me, which surprised them. We discussed those feelings and the benefits of addressing them and moving through them in honest reflection. There were no delusions of grandeur, as I once feared. On the contrary, there was a greater tendency to downgrade themselves and devalue their work and progress.

In course evaluations, some of the responses to ungrading included:

> I have always been very motivated to please teachers and get a "good grade," and not having that as a motivating factor for my effort made me re-evaluate ways in which I can inspire myself to learn for the sake of learning.

> The ungrading was nice in the sense that I was intrinsically motivated to do work, but it does stress me out. I tend to be an over–achiever and anxious, so put in a situation where I am supposed to assess myself is hard because I feel like I can never realistically say I deserve an A or something because there is always more that I could have done.

> I found the more casual approach to teaching with not so much of an emphasis on grading to be so helpful as it diminished some of my stress from my course load and it made the class and practicing for it so much more enjoyable.

> Grading myself throughout the course was really beneficial. I was not stressed out about the class, but still encouraged to do my best work since I knew I would have to evaluate myself.

> I liked how we were focused on ourselves, and self-evaluating in practice assignments and the final.

This choice to ungrade works for me, for now. Perhaps it won't someday, and even if I remain an ungrader, I'm certain that the process and practice will undergo mild to moderate changes in response to my students' experiences. For now, I'll keep listening and learning. That is what feels right for me. Please use the following exercise to feel what's right for you.

Questions for Meditation:

1. There is the potential for both an intellectual and emotional response to each prompt.

   Breathe, feel, speak, write, or draw what comes up. Begin by taking a moment to look at and take in these grades:

   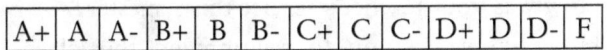

2. What were you taught about grading?
3. How were you graded as a student? Do you identify as an "A" student, "B" student, etcetera?
4. How do you grade as a teacher?
5. What works in your grading rubric, and what might be improved?
6. Do you feel pressure to change your grading based upon the author's experience or the experiences of your colleagues—neither of which are yours?

Chapter 10
Evaluations and Evolutions

With the commodification of higher education, student evaluations can feel like reviews of consumer and product satisfaction:

On a scale of one to five stars, how would you rate your class experience?
How was your teacher's service this semester?
How likely are you to recommend this class to a friend?

As an experienced people pleaser, I strive to ensure that my courses meet expectations, provide quality, value, and convenience, and that I handle complaints with integral communication. And yet, each semester, my heart races as I open the folder of student feedback, steadying myself for a vulnerability hangover. The most practical wisdom I have gleaned is to view Student Evaluations as catalysts for Teaching Evolutions.

Below are ten comments from student evaluations that could, with some humility and introspection, transform one's teaching for the better. So (asking for a friend), what might be the action steps for the teacher receiving this feedback? How could these student observations become opportunities for teaching evolutions?

1. I felt invisible, like just another square on Zoom.
2. It's obvious who [the teacher's] favorite students are.
3. My interest in the subject did not increase.
4. I hated the textbook. Why was it chosen?
5. I wish I'd gone to office hours sooner; that's where I learned the most.
6. I'm looking for [the teacher's] approval, but I could never tell what they really thought of me, so it was hard for me to trust them.
7. Discussion and readings were fine, but I needed like 10% more direct instruction from the professor.
8. I was really challenged by the flow of the class; the responsive teaching was great, but I wanted more structure and instructions for assignments.
9. [The teacher] thinks they know everything!
10. [Their] teaching is like warm buttered bread.

Meditative Practice:

Identify a piece of feedback that you've received about your teaching that you're willing to sit with for a few minutes.

Drop in the thought: "Let me be like water. Let this flow through me."

Notice the movement of your breath, like the movement of a wave.

Allow the wisdom to flow in, and the rest to flow on.

Figure 10.1 Waves (Credit: Andrea Odinov.)

Part II
Exhalation

Chapter 11
Prototypes

As a young teacher, I didn't yet know myself or trust myself. To deal with my imposter syndrome, I relied on my acting skills; I approached the classroom like a stage and performed the role of teacher. I modeled my behavior after the fictional teacher prototypes from my childhood: Miss Stacy, Ms. Frizzle, and Miss Honey.

In Lucy Maude Montgomery's *Anne of Green Gables* (1908), Miss Muriel Stacy is Avonlea School's first female teacher, and she has a reputation for innovation. Her warmth, vivacity, and skill propel Anne to pursue her own career as a writer and teacher. I aspired to be a similarly wholesome and empowering influence on my own students. Whenever possible, I would facilitate whole-body learning and outdoor classes akin to Miss Stacy's physical culture exercises and nature-based lessons. I hoped that my students would find me to be a kindred spirit who believed wholly in their potential and inspired them to be remarkable.

In Ms. Valerie Felicity Frizzle, author Joanna Cole created a pedagogical icon (1986). I loved Ms. Frizzle's eccentricity, humor, and the prevalence of mystery and magic in her classroom. As a teacher of theater, I respected with the Frizz's idea that the best way to know is to *do*. She also seemed infinitely quotable with her catchy aphorisms about learning. And while I didn't have access to a Magic School Bus, I recognized the value of engaging students' imaginations for learning to feel like an extraordinary adventure.

Miss Jennifer Honey, the extraordinary teacher in Roald Dahl's *Matilda* (1988), has a transformative influence on her students. I loved the notion that her eponymous sweetness drew the students to her and that a classroom could be a beehive of energy, creativity, and joy. Her example helped me understand the importance of gentleness, empathy, and warmth as preconditions for Matilda's magical maturation.

It took a decade of practicing acting like a teacher before I truly became an acting teacher. When I finally began to trust my own instincts, not only as a subject-matter expert but also as my unique authentic self, I saw my students do the same. It was far more effort to try to be as good as the prototypes of my youth than just to be myself. The lesson from my students was that they didn't need a performance of good teaching from me, but rather a real person to see and be with them on their own journeys of becoming.

Questions for Meditation:
1. Who were your teaching prototypes, real or fictional?
2. How has your teaching evolved over time?
3. How do your students describe your teaching or mirror your energy in the classroom?

Mantras for Meditation: I am. I am enough, I have enough, I do enough.

Chapter 12
The Wisecracker

He told me that the only reason he signed up for my voice class was because he wanted to learn to do funny voices. "Cartoons, you know?" He was short and tense, with a red wiry beard. He looked like a featherweight boxer, arms up, ready to swing or duck at any moment. And it seemed like he relished testing me with persistent snickering and snarky comments.

One day, I asked him to stick around after class.

Avoiding eye contact, he told me that the exercises we were doing in class were useless… silly… and boring. I felt my breath catch and my ego sting, but I tried to hold space for his frustration. I reminded him that he still had the option to withdraw. He hesitated.

"Or you could stay in the class," I said. "Even though we're not working on funny voices, I do value hearing your voice."

"Really? Usually I'm the problem kid."

"Really. You're observant and witty."

A grin spread beneath his patchy goatee as he dashed out the door.

To our mutual surprise, he didn't drop the course. He was still guarded, but he started listening more and even joined in some of the exercises.

I tried not to take his continued resistance personally, though I struggled to remain patient. So, before seeing him each class, I'd practice a loving-kindness meditation, repeating internally: May he be happy. May he be well. May he be safe. May he be peaceful and at ease.

During finals, I asked each student to identify their takeaway(s) from the course. When his turn in our talking circle arrived, he uncrossed his arms slowly and said quietly: "I learned to let my guard down a bit...and that I don't have to be a wise ass to get attention... Thank you for not giving up on me."

What a relief to us both! Teacher, may you practice patience and experience the quiet joy of witnessing its impact on a student's self-belief and behavior.

Questions for Meditation:
1. When do you feel impatience in the classroom?
2. How do you center yourself when you feel challenged by (student) resistance?

Loving-Kindness Meditation:

May I be happy. May I be well. May I be safe. May I be peaceful and at ease.

May you be happy. May you be well. May you be safe. May you be peaceful and at ease.

May they be happy. May they be well. May they be safe. May they be peaceful and at ease.

Chapter 13
Breakdownthrough

Please be advised: this passage includes a description of an episode of acute anxiety.

It's early fall in an undergraduate acting class. Two students volunteer to demonstrate a strategy for memorizing text. They begin to toss a tennis ball back and forth while repeating their text by rote. If the ball drops or a speaker drops a line, the speaker(s) begin again at the beginning of the text. This dynamic approach engages the actors' bodies and facilitates responsiveness to the partner's delivery of the ball and the text. It can be highly effective…and deeply challenging.

One actor tossed and caught the ball with ease, while their words flowed. The other actor became increasingly tense, stammering, and flushing with embarrassment. They apologized but insisted that they wanted to continue. I encouraged them to breathe and take their time. And yet, with each throw, they began backing up into the corner of the room by the classroom door. When there was nowhere else for them to go but out of the room or toward their partner, I paused the exercise.

"I notice that you backed into the corner. How does it feel to work over there?"

"Oh, I didn't even realize." Their breathing was shallow, and their eyes darted around the room.

"What would it feel like to take up more space?"

And with that, they began to tremble. Panic rippled through their body, and they retreated to their seat, whispering that they just needed space and time to breathe. As someone who has experienced panic attacks, I felt tenderness, empathy, and guilt that I had inadvertently provoked a breakdown. I ran through my mental checklist of Mental Health First Aid and determined that the class should take a ten-minute break. The student and I sat together for a few minutes as their breathing settled and their body relaxed.

> *"No one has ever asked me to take up space before. I've spent my whole life trying to be invisible, while desperate to be seen."*

Their vulnerability and courage sent a ripple through my spine. I had assumed it was the difficulty of the exercise, not the impact of the invitation that had induced panic. Oops.

"I want to be able to work with and through this. How do I do that?"

"Let's try a centering mantra together. As you say each word, you'll gently bring your thumb and one of your fingers together:

> When you touch your index finger, say: PEACE.
>
> When you touch your middle finger, say: BEGINS.
>
> When you touch your ring finger, say: WITH.
>
> When you touch your pinky finger, say: ME."

By focusing our attention on an object outside of ourselves, we both began to feel calmer. And the learning continued.

Much later in the semester, during final scene presentations, this student would have another acute experience of anxiety. But before I could get out of my seat, they waved me off, "I've got this."

I couldn't have been prouder to have been made redundant.

Reflection:

Mindfulness practices cultivate calm through concentration; by anchoring our attention, our cortisol levels lower and things can be seen more clearly. How might you cultivate peace and quietude in your classroom?

Chapter 14
Permission Slips

I noticed that a student was uncomfortable with an idea presented in one of our class's readings. He expressed his reservations cautiously at first, as if he was trying not to offend the article's author.

But it wasn't the author he was worried about, it was me.

He thought that because I had assigned the reading that it reflected my own ideas or beliefs, and he didn't want to contradict or insult me.

So, I asked him and the class of bright-eyed graduate students:

What if the readings were provocations or invitations with which to disagree?
What if each technique and tool we learn about is context-specific?
What if you became the judge of its relevancy and application in your own creative work?

Sometimes even adult learners need permission slips.

Questions for Meditation:
1. What permissions or invitations have benefited your students?

2. What permission do you need as a teacher?
3. How has disagreement or dissent played out in your classroom?

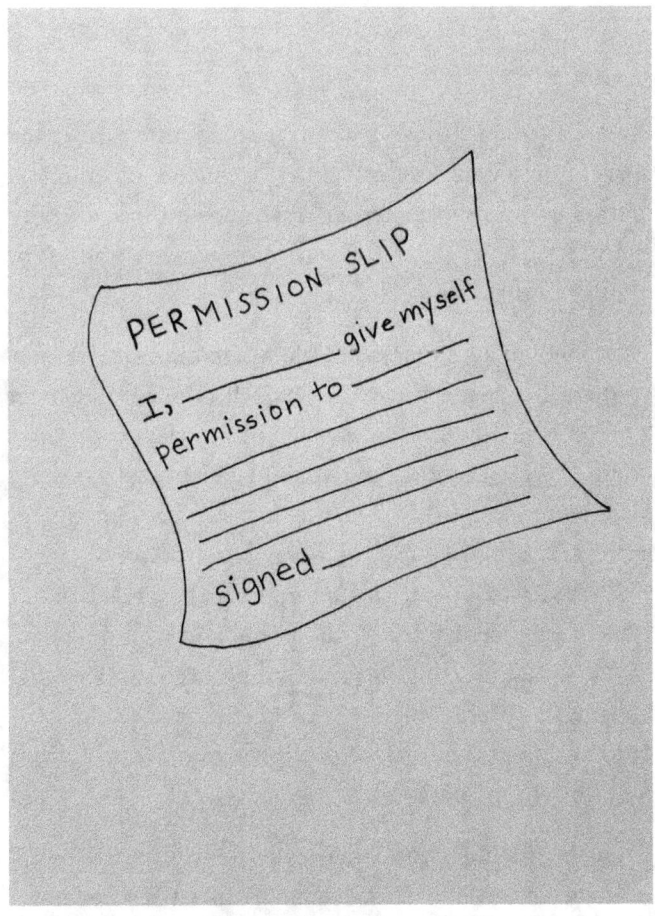

Figure 14.1 Permission slip. (Credit: Andrea Odinov.)

Chapter 15
The Psychology of Apology

As a Canadian, I have a cultural commitment to being sorry. I apologize reflexively, as a matter of etiquette and as a means of interpersonal cooperation. I really thought that I understood the intent and impact of apologies, that is, until I taught Lee.

A bright, anxious, fast-talking undergraduate theater student, Lee made a name for herself in our department as the Queen of Apologies. One of her classmates once counted the number of times Lee apologized in a 90-minute class (≈17). On the surface, Lee's apologies were procedural (sorry for being late), personal (sorry I'm talking too fast), and interpersonal (sorry I didn't remember your name). While polite and well-intended, the over-apologizing became (almost comically) distracting. It presented like a deeply engrained habit or compulsion to apologize for existing, and I wondered why this young person was so very sorry?

Ethically, I understood the scope of my practice and influence as an educator. I have neither the knowledge nor clinical skills to provide psychological support. However, I felt a responsibility to become a more trauma-informed educarer[1]. I knew that human nervous systems automatically respond to threat or danger by running to safety (flight), aggressively facing the threat (fight), or reactively immobilizing (freeze). A fourth response, coined by therapist Pete Walker, is to avoid conflict through appeasing or forestalling the danger (fawn). In this paradigm, over-apologizing is a fawning strategy for self-preservation.

It was possible that, due to some prior trauma (personal or educational), Lee had learned to use apology as her primary tool for social survival. And in educational and theatrical settings, where power imbalances and harsh criticism are often present, I could empathize with Lee's need to preemptively apologize to protect herself from conflict, discomfort, or rejection.

Through meditating on Lee's behavior, I recognized an opportunity to model more mindful and meaningful apologies. Here are a few ways to integrate:

1. In your community agreement, consider including an Oops, Ouch, and Whoa framework for difficult conversations.
2. As a closing ritual, each student can offer a statement of Appreciation, an Apology, or an Aha moment.
3. If something feels unresolved between classes and you desire repair or reconciliation, try practicing the Ho'oponopono Prayer. Repeat internally: "I'm sorry. Please forgive me. Thank you. I love you."

Note
1 An educator who cares.

Chapter 16
Ahimsa

Some of my happiest teaching days are working with singers. One semester, I had the pleasure of coaching a young mezzo soprano whose voice sounded like warm golden honey. Through our time together, she hoped to develop her range and her power, to belt higher and with less strain.

I love this phase of a singer's development. It can be scary, exciting, and inspiring to hear/feel a voice experience new notes, tones, and sensations.

To our in-class coaching session, the singer brought "Quiet" by Jonathan Reid Gealt, a terrific piece to explore her goals. She sang through it once in "a just for fun run," as her classmates listened in rapt attention with tears in their eyes. When she finished, the room was quiet for a moment, before erupting in thunderous applause.

She apologized for not being fully warmed up. (Evidently, it's hard to find places to nap and places to sing at the top of your lungs.) I began with affirmation:

"Dear one, you have nothing to prove and everything to share. Would you like to keep working?"

"Yes, please."

Consent established; I asked her to revisit the song's bridge (a difficult section in the middle of the song). I hoped to integrate more Head, Neck, and Torso Anchoring from the Estill Voice Training System, which dynamically engages larger muscles to support the vocal effort.

"As you try that passage again, how would it feel to open your arms wide and lean your head back?"

She tried it, and her voice bloomed. "Wow, I feel powerful, and I sound so loud!"

Then she tried again and faltered. "I'm a little scared. My voice feels more tired than usual."

I wanted her to trust herself and her instrument. I wanted her to integrate this new possibility into her body. "May I place my hand on the back of your head, to help you maintain that engagement while you try again?"

She nodded, familiar with our department's practice of establishing informed consent before instructional touch.

I placed my hand on the back of her head as if cradling her skull and offering gentle pressure. But my proximity and the pressure to produce a certain result changed something for her. I sensed her resistance through her shallow breath and slightly quivering knees. She stepped away from me:

"No, I don't want to try it right now."

I felt the observing students' concern and curiosity. So many of them have been trained, as young theater students, to say "yes, and" to each invitation or direction from a teacher. But this student was practicing something else: flexing her bodily autonomy. In revoking consent, she re-established her boundaries and authority in her practice. So, I stepped back:

"It's awesome that you know that and expressed that. I call that a Vocal Ahimsa, an act of nonviolence towards yourself. I heard you say earlier that you don't feel fully rested or warmed up today. What would you like to do?"

"I want to try it one more time on my own today."

She tried again, and her old habit joined her. But when she finished, she said:

"It was too big a reach for me today, but I'll keep stretching. Thank you for letting me trust my body's pace."

Questions for Meditation:
1. Where might the practice of ahimsa (nonviolence) be relevant in your practice?
2. What would it feel like to take a couple of centering breaths before saying "yes, and" or "no, but" to an invitation?
3. Does your workplace have an instructional touch policy? How do you establish boundaries and consent in your creative spaces?

Chapter 17
Whole Body Yes

It's the class after the Ahisma discovery. Another student shyly sidles up to me:

"What happened last class was so cool to watch! I loved hearing [the singer's] voice evolve with that new technique. And she was so self-aware! …You know, I don't think I've ever had a director or choreographer ask me what I want to do next. I'm used to being told what to do and how to do it and my job is figuring out why. So, can I ask you about this thing you said at the end of the last class? About noticing our Whole-Body Yeses? What did you mean by that?"

I breathe deeply. The student is asking something important. I try to put my attention fully on her, to attune to her energy and her need for knowing.

"I imagine the body as a magnet, pulling us towards what's true. So, sometimes direction and instruction can come from within like hunches or sudden signals. As artists, we learn to listen to the body's wanting muscles that help us to take creative action. Your listening, and the strength of your wanting muscles, will deepen with practice."

"What are my wanting muscles?"

"Well, we might notice, when we're experiencing a yes signal that we sense an opening, an expansion, or a warmth inside. Maybe your breath deepens, or you experience a sigh of relief. For me, my jaw unwinds, and I feel my shoulders drop a little. More flow, you know?"

Her head bobs. I sense her softening, remembering.

"Our body might give us other signals like sensations of constriction, tension, pulling back/down/away, or a sense of heaviness. Those are our signals for no, you know? Those are also moments that, if ignored or over-ridden, can become issues in our tissues."

She stands. Looks down in astonishment. And when she looks up at me, I sense that her Inner Guidance System, her great magnet, had just nudged her toward something new, something true.

Questions and Practices for Meditation:

1. Would you like to try a somatic meditation?

    Drop your head to your chest.

    Wrap your arms around yourself (like a big hug).

    Invite the thought: "I am meant to live in peace."

    Take five deep breaths.

    Notice what sensations arise.

    Release.

2. As a practice for discernment: consider a creative or pedagogical decision that you are making. Identify two possible courses of action and hold them (imaginatively) in your palms. Observe the body's wisdom arising through breath, flow, temperature, or tension. How does it feel to hold each thought?

Chapter 18
Hover and Hunker

A conversation with Jenn Robbins, artist, educator, and graduate student.

Jenn, when we were in rehearsal together last year, I marveled at your creative process. There were two practices that I would especially love to learn more about. In your work, what does 'hovering' mean?

I was introduced to hovering and hunkering by my teachers, Stephen Wangh and Wendy Vanden Heuvel, through their psychophysical Grotowski-based practices. Hovering for me is not limited to my acting practice or teaching. I often find myself hovering in life and parenting, as well. Meaning, I encourage myself and my children to practice hovering in the unknown and trusting that not knowing is ok. That the next thing will be here in a moment, and we can deal with it, even play with it—whether pleasant or unpleasant. We can learn to hover when we don't know what to do and let the "what now?" question be answered through a process of cultivating curiosity and trust. [We] therefore become more comfortable with receiving and responding instinctually… It is highly creative. You become stronger and more able to stand the unknown, stand it, and stand in it.

What an act of creative courage!

If you plan every single thing you are going to do, you will never be surprised. I like being surprised when I act. In life, not so much. I wish I did like it, and so that's one reason why I like to practice my ability to hover in life—to stand the unknown—maybe even embrace it. The more we can cultivate curiosity, the more we're able to stand in the unknown, to bear that feeling, however uncomfortable (or scary) it may be. Asking "what now" can become interesting. Surprising and original and connected images and feelings can arise by being willing to hover in the unknown and waiting for what's next. Trusting something is coming is very exciting and looking forward to interacting with what's next cultivates a kind of joy that is desirable in acting, and life.

I could see that joy in you and in your work! Jenn, what does it mean to 'hunker'?

I like the idea of hunkering down with my thoughts after an exercise or rehearsal, to gather my impressions of how it went: what I did, what my partner did, what worked, and what didn't.

Ah, so it's an independent practice for reflecting and synthesizing the creative experience.

Yes. Hunkering helps actors receive their impressions of their work, and pragmatically track what went on, so that they are developing a mindful acting practice and can keep building on what they did or improve it. It's logical, methodical work.

I've seen other actors process their learning verbally, through journaling or meditation. This seems like a more physical practice; is squatting or crouching an important aspect of the creative hunker?

I let my students know whether they want to crouch in the corner or stand or sit, it's no matter. The hunker can be done in any way physically, it just must be done to keep that mind-body-spirit connection going and help you improve. It's not judgmental, just observational, evaluative. Plus, and I think this is important, it puts value on the work the student just did, without getting precious about it.

Thank you for sharing your art and your heart, Jenn! I'm excited to explore hovering and hunkering.

Questions for Meditation:
1. How might you, or your students, practice the creative hover?
2. What does hunkering look like for you? How do you pause, withdrawing from habits and the constant barrage of stimulation, to process your life? A class? A rehearsal?
3. In your teaching, what is the ratio of preparation to improvisation?

Chapter 19
Spoons

One year, a beloved student gifted me with two beautifully carved wooden spoons. I was honored, and a bit perplexed, by the gift. She explained that the most valuable lesson from our time together was an anecdote that I shared in her graduate acting class:

> As a young acting fellow at the Shakespeare Theatre Company, my first production was William Congreve's *The Way of the World*. I played Betty, a servant at the chocolate house, and I dedicated myself to stirring, pouring, and carrying mugs of chocolate. One performance, as I carried the serving tray downstage, I tripped over my fabulous hoop skirt. The metal spoons I was carrying clattered onto the wooden deck; it was so loud the principal actors stopped speaking. In my naïveté and embarrassment, I blushed and fled upstage leaving the spoons on the ground. Mortified that I had interrupted the scene and pulled focus, I apologized to the actors at intermission. One of them kindly explained to me that dropping the spoons wasn't a big deal. The more important thing to learn was to pick them up: acting requires that we respond fully to what is actually happening in the moment, not denying the truth of what is.

For my acting students, the Spoon Story became a valuable teaching parable. It signified the importance of present-moment awareness and responsiveness. It also revealed that our perceived foibles and failures are moments of sharing our full humanity; such authenticity cultivates trust and connection onstage and in classes.

In this light, my perceived failure presented, for both me and my future students:

> *__F__eedback that __A__llowed us to go __I__nside and __L__earn.*

Questions for Meditation:
1. What was the culture of risk and failure in your educational experience?
2. In what ways have your own educational experiences helped you define the atmosphere that you would like to create for others?
3. What does it mean to you to share your selfhood in service of learning?

Chapter 20
I Need a Champion

In the nadir of the pandemic, we were weary and dispirited. Educating and educaring online felt hollow, lonely, and sometimes impossible. As the antidote to our despair, we created a digital story-catching survey, inviting our student community to share some wisdom with our teaching community. Below we share a sample of notable responses:

In your experience, what are the most helpful things that teachers do?

- "Believe in you! Even if you're not the most skilled, letting you know that discipline in learning, even not in your chosen field, is worth it all, no matter how frustrating."
- "Always being kind; yet challenging."
- "Teachers can spark something in a student that they never dreamed they would/could be interested in."
- "Encourage, even when wrong answers are given."
- "Inspire students to try their best to improve their understanding of subject matter being presented."

What are the most harmful things that teachers do?

- "Assume they know everything."
- "Ignore the needs of a student."
- "Dismiss a dream or skill that they might not have the most aptitude for. Talent (in any field) cannot be determined until a student has a set of skills. What you do with your skills is your measure of talent. I know some technically brilliant [artists] that don't have an ounce of personal investment in their work."

What assumptions do teachers make about you?

- "That I am confident because I am not afraid to question or debate, when really I am compensating for insecurity."
- "That I can learn easily by reading instructions."

What do you wish your teachers knew?

- "I wish all teachers knew how difficult it is to teach a classroom of students that are at all different levels of knowledge."
- "Most lecture classes are often phoned in, year after year, with little time to veer off syllabus. The weeks just sort of crank by, heading toward the final exam, and the almighty grade. If you get it, you get it. If you don't, you don't."
- "How to lead you to an answer without simply providing it."
- "That I am easily discouraged."

Questions for Meditation:

1. In your experience, what are the most helpful things that teachers do?
2. What are the most harmful things that teachers do?
3. What assumptions do teachers make about you?
4. What do you wish your teachers knew?
5. Was there someone who championed your learning? How did they impact your journey?

Walking Meditation:

Consider taking a walk with the following question:
Along your path, what lessons have you offered your teachers?

Figure 20.1 A path. (Credit: Andrea Odinov.)

Part III
Transformation

Chapter 21
Whose Need Is It Anyway?

I was teaching Voice at a well-regarded acting conservatory in Los Angeles. My classes were based on Fitzmaurice Voicework®, structured across three levels (Voice 1, 2, 3), and students were at significantly varied stages in their training. In any given class, I might have one student with years of previous voice and bodywork, working alongside another who was new to actor training in general, and perhaps, even more new to their own body.

Fitzmaurice Voicework® is somatic work, and like with any type of bodywork, discoveries can be unexpectedly thrilling, pleasurable, informative, confusing, frightening, and possibly painful—depending on how the student perceives the experience, and how the experience is guided by, guess who? The teacher.

As my students were exploring body and breath release work, I was walking around the studio, observing, and guiding, sometimes with words and sometimes with physical adjustments. I noticed one student in a dynamic effort that I wanted to adjust. It wasn't that the student was in danger of hurting himself, but rather, I could see where the body was bracing, what might facilitate release—and I wanted to foster that awareness in him, so he could have a deeper experience. I approached.

I don't think I made it within three feet of him, when he simultaneously shooed me away both with his arm and his sound, "*T-S-S-Z-ZZZ!!!*," which loosely translated to *LEAVE ME BE.*

How dare he! defensively and incredulously thought my ego.

I was the teacher! I knew what he was doing "wrong." I could see the body, I could see the blocks and bracing, and I could see what might free up the energetic flow. And I was older than him! And if I were a male teacher, he wouldn't have—and, and, and…

…*aaand*…he wanted to sort it out himself. This was a lovely student who was always respectful, not the least bit sexist, and a joy to teach. This was his third course with me. He was curious. He wanted to explore everything that I was seeing but *for himself*. Ultimately, that's the point, isn't it? To train the actor to be curious, to venture into the unknown, to explore the discomfort, to learn, to see, and to have their own agency. To take our pedagogy and make it meaningful and useful to them, because eventually, the teacher and student must let the other go.

At that time, thankfully, it took a split second for me to recognize my ego's reaction and find that sweet space between reaction and response. I remembered my purpose as the teacher and genuinely appreciated his uncensored expression of desired self-sufficiency. After the release work, when students were invited to share any observations or raise questions, he communicated his experience, and I did too. There were no hard feelings; there was no battle for control. We even laughed about the spontaneous sound he made to shoo me away.

He taught me.

In that moment with him, I realized the following lesson:

I needed to go to my student more than he needed me to.

Perhaps I needed to feel like I was "doing something." Perhaps I needed control. Perhaps I needed validation for what I saw and intuited. This was not a new lesson for me, in theory. During my Fitzmaurice Voicework® Teacher Certification Program, I specifically remember one of my brilliant teachers addressing this very topic. We were to consider whether in a particular moment, the student needed us, or did we need the student? We explored the difference between being with a student in presence and curiosity, as opposed to being with a student and looking for things to fix without regard for the student's experience. So, I *knew* all of that, and, in that moment, forgot. Thank goodness for our students, who remind us—if we let them.

My mind traveled beyond the classroom. At that time, I was a church choir singer, and during a rehearsal, one of the singers with physical challenges fell. The other singers, out of love and concern, rushed to her aid, surrounding her. Recalling my experience with my student, I asked her, "What do you need right now?" to which she firmly replied, "I need a minute and some space" so that she could help herself up again. The well-intended group returned to their seats, but some did look at me as though I were a monster who just did what Jesus certainly *wouldn't* do.

I thought about how I heard it said that handing someone a tissue subconsciously tells them to stop crying—when what they really need is to cry. That maybe just being with, providing that space for them to release is what they need but might not be able to communicate. I wonder if asking for a tissue because your feelings are leaking out of your nose is a different experience than being handed one, pre-emptively. And when is the right time? Do you wait until I have begun to wipe my eyes and nose with my own clothing? ... Or do you say preciously, *"I have a tissue for you, but I'm going to withhold it in honor of your needs, in this safe space I've created for both you and the contents of your sinuses..."*

This isn't an easy area to live in. We're not machines. We are sensitive, empathic humans, who want to connect and help. And if we've found our home in the arts, then those traits are often heightened. We don't want to appear callous if someone has fallen, or is crying, and we certainly don't want to be a teacher who is perceived as "doing nothing." We often consider what *we* would need, and project that onto another, assuming our needs are the same.

The yoga studio I belong to offers chips (think poker, not potato) that a student can place at the corner of their mat if they don't wish to be touched. I like this idea, and I now incorporate a similar practice in my classroom. Since I keep forgetting to purchase poker chips, I ask my students to use a gentle hand gesture (as if to signal "stop") if they sense my approach and wish to be alone with their experience. If allowed to approach, I do ask my students for permission before making physical adjustments, and I try (and fail) to only offer adjustments if I see something that might be injurious, or so habitual that it requires additional support in unlearning its unhelpful habit.

Some students want and need attention. Some students want and need full autonomy. Some students will not communicate their needs to you, and others may not be able to identify their needs until the exact moment in which they arise. Some students (and teachers) confuse "want" with "need."

I'm not suggesting that we teach (or live) in a world where we just watch someone fall without lending a hand, watch someone cry without lending a tissue or an embrace, or watch a student struggle to deepen their experience without guiding them to that next level... however, we, as teachers, need to be in touch with whose need it is. If any action or interaction I take with my students fulfills my need, yet ignores theirs, then it's only serving me.

This is not easy. We must be prepared to fail at this many times and to be gentle with ourselves as we do. Our task is not to be the perfect teacher, any more than the task for our students is to be the perfect student. In fact, the desire to be the "perfect student" is what will contribute to a student directly avoiding their own needs to be compliant. As a beloved teacher of mine said, "If a student tries to please me, I can't teach them."

Questions for Meditation:

1. How can you assess whether your actions are serving your need or your student's need? Is there a possibility of both, coexisting?
2. Can you recall a moment in your life when your need was overridden or ignored by well-meaning humans? (Teacher, parent, friend?)
3. How can we teach our students to be aware of and express their needs in a way that is both helpful for them and for us as their teachers?

Chapter 22
Lessons from my Dream Students

First, a bit of title clarification: "Dream Students" does not mean those stellar students that are just a dream to work with but, rather, students who appear in the expression of my subconscious as I slumber. Oh, and by "dreams," I mean nightmares. As in *The Teacher's Nightmare*.

Have you had The Actor's Nightmare? It comes in many forms, but mine involves being in a play I've performed before, but so long ago I can't remember any of my lines. I'm not even in costume, and after panicking backstage for what feels like forever in dream time, I take the stage and improvise my way around the set, just making things up, speaking gibberish, and wanting it to be over. It's awful, and luckily, I haven't had one of those in ages. Instead, my subconscious replaced acting with teaching.

I'm in the classroom and my usual roster of 14 students has morphed into what feels like 140 students. They're everywhere. Total chaos. No one is sitting quietly looking over lines, scrolling through their phone, or chatting with a nearby friend. They are literally climbing the walls, running amok, and it's really, really, loud. I try to draw their attention. I feel my dream voice pushed, tight, and shrill as it screeches, "Listen to meeeeeeee!" No one does. I physically stop students, one by one, grabbing their shoulders and shouting "BE QUIET!" at them. No one is quiet. I look for my syllabi, and I only have my copy. I rush out of the room and run frantically through campus trying to find a copy machine. Time is racing. My heart is racing. By the time I return to my classroom, time has run out and class is over.

When I first began teaching, I used to have that sweet little dream before the start of each academic year. It kind of freaked me out, both in frequency and feeling. There were obvious themes of control and preparation, but what really disturbed me was my dream-self: (a) grabbing my students (something I'd never, *ever* do), and (b) screaming at them. Not being listened to created notable dream-anger in me, and there was such an emotional hangover from those dreams that they are some of the few dreams I remember to this day.

Recently, I realized in meditation that I hadn't had the teacher's nightmare in a while. In truth, I couldn't remember the last time I had it. I gave myself a little energetic pat on the back at how I must have resolved the issues my dream students symbolized, and isn't healing and growth magical? I swear, every single time I have a self-congratulatory thought like that, the Universe says, "Oh yeah? Watch this…" A night or two later, the nightmare returned with similar themes, but the architect had tinkered with the matrix.

I'm not in a classroom. I'm in an unidentifiable space, like a large performance venue lobby, with various seating arrangements that break up vast areas of floor, but unlike anywhere I've ever been. It's very futuristic and abstract in its design. Again, it feels like there are a million students. I'm not grabbing or screaming at them this time, thank goodness, but I do try to vocally gather them. They oblige. I introduce some sort of theater game or exercise, and it's an experience that I want them to spend time with. They begin, but moments later, they start to leave the playing floor. Some wander off, and others gather in the seating areas to socialize. Now I feel like I'm herding cats. There's disinterest and willfulness and each time I shepherd a student back to the project, another one leaves. As I move to retrieve more students, one student whom I just taught in my waking life, stops me. He touches his face, points to his nasolabial folds (where the cheeks crease when smiling), and tells me I need to apply lotion there.

I awoke completely confounded. My students have taught me to let go of the control I perceived necessary in my nascent years of teaching. I can't control what they learn, how they learn, or *if* they learn—all I can do is give them information, guide them, and create a space and relationship in which they can communicate with me how their journey is faring. They're not always going to listen to me. (*I* don't always listen to me.) I repeat information as much as they need, even if it was said moments ago. And if they're noisy, be it from an activity or social chatter, I don't try to overpower their noise with my voice. Instead, I turn the lights off and on once—something I learned when visiting a School for the Deaf—or I'll use an agreed-upon gesture. So, why was I having the teacher's nightmare again after having been free of it for years? What needed to be worked through now?

The dream's futuristic, abstract, unrecognizable teaching space represented the sudden shifts of newness in education I'd experienced: online pedagogy and learning, which involved a crash course in new technology; Diversity, Equity, and Inclusion practices, that necessitated an honest assessment of my perspective, pedagogy, and materials; and teaching Generation Z, who were understandably different from their Millennial predecessors. The theatrical classroom exploration I introduced symbolized both unfamiliar and experimental frontiers in academia and professional projects of mine (including this book.) Perhaps the students milling in and out of the theatrical exercise represented my feeling ungrounded in my new ventures, and my energy dispersed. I wanted validation from my dream students that what I was creating, and offering was worthy of existence and experience. At first, I was perplexed about the face and lotion moment. I assumed that was about my superficial physical aging. But upon deeper reflection, it symbolized aging in the form of mental rigidity against inevitable changes in pedagogy, in students, and in myself.

So, I'm going to meditate on that and breathe into feelings of imposter syndrome, limited professional and personal self-worth, risk-taking, and yes, aging, in both body and mind.

Do you experience the following? Breathe with each and see where it lands for you.

1. "Imposter Syndrome" or perceptions in professional and personal self-worth.
2. Pedagogical risks vs. what you know and what feels safe.
3. Mental rigidity and resistance in teaching.

Oh, one last thought I'd like to share having known the dream student who pointed to his face, specifically, the smile folds. An additional interpretation is that it was a reminder to smile. To relax, trust my students, trust myself, and teach both from and with love—love of self, love of them, and love of this beautifully bizarre vocation.

Meditative Practice:
Inhale deeply (I love...)
Exhale completely (I trust...)

Chapter 23
Teaching through Chaos

Spring semester, 2020, before "The Great Pause": I was teaching an intermediate voice class focused on Fitzmaurice Voicework® to B.A. Theater students. In the room with me was a group of the most curious, sensitive, and willing humans, some of whom had a prior introduction to this highly somatic voice training, and others who were relatively new to it. I felt like I'd won the teacher's lottery with this group. The energy in the room was powerful, and these sensitive students acknowledged and appreciated that they created this energy together. Physical dynamic efforts opened doors for emotional release—sometimes as contagious laughter and other times as quiet tears. I supported them, they supported each other, and they supported themselves with presence, listening, and touch that were respectful and consensual.

Touch. Touch of a hand, a spine to another spine, touch of vibration. Vibration through voice became information for them, and a way to soothe, connect, and interact. We worked in a large space that felt intimate with fourteen breathing bodies lying side-by-side on fourteen tumbling mats we attached to one giant, blue, supportive ground. The studio was not a "smart room" so often we huddled together around my 13" laptop to watch videos I use as teaching tools. It was not unusual for them to sit with their arms around each other, or to lean against each other for seated support.

The theme of our last class before we left for Spring Break was Grounding. This would prep them for the unit upon our return, which was to be: "Through Chaos Comes Clarity."

Cue the COVID-Chaos.

The following is an excerpt from my teaching journal written directly after that first zoom class:

Intermediate Voice Online, Day 1:

Emotional. Students sad, stressed, anxious. Can't be in the same space with them. As each one enters the "room" I feel varying colors of disappointment, hopelessness, confusion, and doubt. Once we're all together (minus one who is asleep on the other side of the world) I feel them, yet I feel so separated from them.

We check in. We breathe. We can't make eye contact.

Looking into the webcam brings no reciprocal sensation.

We begin our body/voice warm-up sequence. I hear breath. I hear sound. The audio makes them sound robotic, fractured, in and out. Then, I hear crying— soft, gentle release of a tense body that's been through so much. I can't go to the student. I can't offer supportive, guiding touch.

All I can say, is "I hear you."

I'm crying. I'm teaching through a shaking voice and closing throat. Trying to find my ribs, structure my breathing, allow my experience to come through my voice without being overcome by my experience. I feel affected by my students. I feel stuck in my chair. I feel I failed.

As the course continued, we adjusted. They were very vocal about what worked for them and what didn't, but we continued to work, nonetheless. Office hour sessions that began as "I just want to talk," moved into, "I want to work on my breath when I'm recording a self-tape." In working with the technology, the course, which began as voice primarily for stage, became more geared for screen. Videos of close-ups on actors who were breathing-thinking-feeling-reacting became starting points for discussion and exploration. It was not the course I intended to teach, but it was interesting to see it unfold into something new.

And it wasn't all smooth and seamless, either. There were days when they were angry. One student expressed anger in a weekly assigned journal. The student wrote that my instructions during one class felt *really* unhelpful, and there were no holds barred in expressing this. We scheduled an appointment and talked about it in a healthy, constructive, and mutually respectful way; anger became a growth opportunity for this student and, for me, a moment of reflection regarding my contribution to the experience. There were days when students were barely hanging on emotionally. Days when one or two didn't want their cameras on, not because they were "up to something," but because it made them feel incredibly self-conscious, and distracted to watch themselves working. We had a ton of technical issues, and some students did not have space conducive to learning. Friday and sometimes Saturday nights were when I'd meet with one student asynchronously because of a significant time difference; my voice tired at the end of the day, their voice tired from waking up only moments before our sessions. I'll never forget how this student, isolated from friends, classmates, and normal life, always made it a point to ask me if I was ok, and how was I holding up.

I live alone. When I say "alone," I mean without another human. I do live with a very vocal cat, who took pleasure in presenting herself to the webcam during class on more than one occasion, but... Something I enjoy about being on campus, is that following class, you can choose to process, rest, and reflect in the privacy of your office, or there is the option to visit a colleague and share. I am so very fortunate to feel that my colleagues are like family to me. Sure, we annoy and frustrate each other at times, but there is always, without fail, more than one person to listen, hold space, laugh, or take a walk to get coffee and debrief with. To say that experience was missed during this remote teaching would be an understatement. (To say that I missed my hour-long commute, however, would be an overstatement, if not a bold-faced lie.)

The end of the semester came and soon to follow were the course evaluations, which I think all professors were a little apprehensive about. But they proved very helpful. Students were honest about units that they enjoyed online and ones that they didn't. They were generous in their comments and understanding that I didn't choose this teaching modality any more than they chose this manner of learning. The complimentary comments (from a personal note and evaluations) that follow are *not* put forth in praise of myself, as I credit *what* I teach far more than my pedagogy. They are here to offer insight into what I realized students value, which is something that continues to surprise me, even after years of teaching:

> Our class is the only class left that I feel present for. My participation feels as though it matters, and I am still learning new things about myself each day. Going forward, I look to explore why this class works. Why I feel that I am actually in a room of people interacting, while in other classes it feels like shouting into the void... Being present with someone over a computer is a new skill, and perhaps it can strengthen in person interactions as well.
>
> I really appreciate how you can be the authoritative figure, but still be a human with emotions, experiencing everything.

I will always remember this class as the thing that grounded me during quarantine and brought me peace.

Students want to feel that they are recognized and significant. Being seen and heard, with full permission to be…even angry—especially at their teachers, whether it's misdirected or not, is important. Their professor's expertise is certainly important, but I've learned that sometimes being human is more so. I'd thought I'd failed them when I couldn't "get it together" while teaching them that first online day. But they valued that. Perhaps it validated and normalized their feelings. Perhaps it taught them how to find voice while experiencing emotion (something they always ask how to do).

Even though there are unique opportunities that teaching through a computer can provide, I can honestly admit that I do prefer being in an actual physical space with students where eye contact can be shared, touch can be given and received, and voices can be heard and felt. But what I'm taking with me from this experience is that resistance to "new" is normal, humanity is valuable, and yes, through chaos comes clarity.

Figure 23.1 An embrace. (Credit: Andrea Odinov.)

Chapter 24
When the Teacher Is Not Alright

Student: Is Andrea ok?
Administrator: She's going through a lot right now ...
Student: Oh ... *Why is she taking it out on us?*

I heard of this exchange about a year after it happened. I heard it with my heart, and it hurt. The administrator (who was also a friend) knew this was highly unusual feedback for me and did not report it to me at the time. It only came up during a social gathering when I was reflecting on how challenging it had been at that time for me to even show up to work, let alone teach. I expressed gratitude for the support from those at the conservatory, whose hearts had held space for me.

"Please take responsibility for the energy you bring into our room" was written on my syllabus, and I read those words aloud on the first day of the semester. This invitation inspired a thoughtful discussion with my students about how our energy affects us, affects each other, and how we take responsibility for what we bring into the room. Students were assured that they never had to force positive energy, as I do not subscribe to a "good vibes only" mindset or space.

Instead, it was a request to be aware of one's energy, name it (if possible), own it, and not misdirect it at anyone. Heads nodded, chests lifted, and smiles emerged. We breathed in agreement.

Each class that semester began with a check-in and space for announcements, questions, or anything anyone needed to give voice to. One day a student offered that they were feeling "really negative," that they had experienced a "bad morning," and, in honor of our agreement, they wanted to say that out loud. It was lovely to witness; their classmates held space without giving the student advice or trying to change their experience. The student remarked at the end of the class how their energy had shifted, and they no longer felt as they had two hours ago. They appreciated that experience.

I fully understood in theory, the agreement applied to me as well. I *thought* I took responsibility for my energy but, for the first time in my life, I didn't quite know what I felt. I felt everything and nothing, everywhere and nowhere, and tried to act and perform what later revealed itself to be a rather unconvincing role.

There was chaos at home. Sleepless nights and stressful days of constant groundlessness. Using my voice to teach temporarily quieted my own inner voice, which desperately tried to solve my problems from every conceivable angle. Nothing worked. Nothing felt safe. Nothing was in my control. Living in the City of Angels (whose residents all travel in cars, all at the same time) I was usually grateful for my ten-minute commute to school. But on those tough mornings, I needed a longer scene change from where I had been to where I was going. I knew I wasn't ready to be with and guide other humans, any more than I was ready to be with and guide myself. I dragged this self up the stairs to my classroom.

At home, I didn't have control, so I sought it in the classroom. I perceived tardiness and lack of attendance as personal disrespect and lack of commitment. I perceived lack of lesson retention as being unheard, and unvalued. I perceived that what I experienced in my personal life was mirrored by my professional life. I perceived everything as truth, and I responded, at times, harshly to those truths. And then I felt guilty because "do no harm" is a part of the Hippocratic Oath that I believe educators should swear by too.

I tried to compensate. I breathed a lot. I arrived at my room early and meditated. I greeted my students with a forced smile and tried to focus on them. They asked me how I was, but I lied. I didn't want my problems to be their problems, and I didn't want my problems to be real in the first place—which they would be if I gave them voice. I didn't want them to know that I had cried moments before they arrived. During the two 30-minute breaks in my six-hour teaching day, instead of giving my body the food and rest it needed, I sent texts and made phone calls in need of information which might sort out my personal life and somehow create momentary ease—at least enough to buoy me through the next class. At that time, I really didn't know what I needed, and I really didn't know how to ask for it.

Why didn't I just take a "sick day?" Sometimes I did, but I didn't want to make a habit of it, for practical, professional, and personal reasons. "Power through!" had been my mentality to avoid the guilt that would come with failing to show up. My mind made a choice, and my body chose differently. I'm normally the type of person who *maybe* catches a cold once a year, but at that time I caught two cold-like things in two months.

Fortunately, like everything in life and even life itself, that chapter of my story was temporary. Eventually, I breathed again and began to heal. The next semester felt different; I was no longer sleepless or groundless, and my energy was focused and revitalized. I was able to be responsible for my energy, and I could be present with my students. My previous perceptions about being disrespected, unheard, and unvalued were gone. It was time to play again.

"Class is much more positive this semester," said a returning student after class. It was said very sweetly and sincerely, and yet I felt the sting of shame. *Had I been found out?* I took a shuddered breath and confessed that I had been "going through a lot" last semester and apologized for how it affected the class. They looked at me sympathetically and said, "Well, sometimes students don't help. We can be annoying."

I nodded gratefully but remained steadfast in my acknowledgment of my contribution to the previous semester's dynamic.

I'm moved by those students who gave me grace while simultaneously using their voice to speak up about what didn't feel right. That is, in truth, part of what I teach them in a voice class. I see that now, and that feels good.

Despite what I consider to be the most challenging and painful period of my life thus far, despite my inability at that time to be the kind of teacher I aspire to and know myself to be, and despite the pain, however mild, my students felt because of my energy, the world did not end.

Please give yourself grace. Give your students grace.

Figure 24.1 A narrow cliff. (Credit: Andrea Odinov.)

Questions for Meditation:

1. How do we take responsibility for the energy we bring into a room?
2. How can we both fulfill our responsibilities and manage ourselves in difficult times? How do we teach our students to do the same?
3. How do you treat the transitions in your teaching day?

Figure 24.2 An open door. (Credit: Andrea Odinov.)

Chapter 25
Unspeakable Wounds

Let's leave academia for a moment and go to the professional world. Here is where I also work as a professional voice, speech, and dialect coach. In Equity houses and sound stages, I no longer have formal students but rather collaborative colleagues who have hired me to support their creative work. They still can and do teach me some of the most important lessons because it's here that I witness how their theater education prepared them, shaped them, and, even at times, harmed them.

For over a decade, I have enjoyed the opportunity to dialect coach plays by black playwrights, directed by various black directors, especially one with whom I've worked the most consistently. In my ignorance during those earliest projects, I never thought a thing of being a white dialect coach, coaching black voices. When I'm asked to coach, I coach, and I loved working with this director and their casts so much that whenever Sidney requested me, I always said yes. I had given it enough thought, however, to know that my sound samples for dialect work should be culturally appropriate native speakers; that *I* should not be the speech model, nor prescribe the speech for a black voice, or any voice, really. I knew my job was to gather resources, to work descriptively rather than prescriptively, and to facilitate the physical realization of sounds. Each time I worked with Sidney, I first reviewed my resources with them, we discussed which sound samples felt right for the play, and only with their approval were those resources presented to the cast. The collaboration and the trust I felt from Sidney has created one of my most cherished professional relationships.

The first time I knew I had much more to learn when an actor said to me with a laugh: "Are you gonna teach us how to talk black?" This happened in one of the earliest shows I coached for Sidney. It was one of those rare moments when I found myself speechless. My first thoughts were, *Goodness, no! I would never! I'm just sharing examples of black voices from this specific time and place and facilitating that accent acquisition for you...if you need it...* But I froze because I began to see how true a concern that was, despite the light-hearted delivery, and I wanted to respond in a way that honored that concern. I can't remember exactly what my response was, but it was some semblance of my thoughts, and I'm sure they noticed how incredibly awkward I was. I never forgot that question, and I continue to think about it and everything it represents to this day. And at the end of the rehearsal process, this same actor gave me the warmest hug that I can still feel to this day.

A few years later, I was thrilled to sit at the table with Sidney and their cast again, about to embark on another theatrical journey. We had met a month prior to the first rehearsal to review my research and have conversations as we always had. A few rehearsals later, I gave my dialect presentation, feeling Sidney's support from the other end of the table but also feeling something else directly seated in front of me.

Ellis looked down the entire time. Arms were folded across their chest, their mouth held tight. It was one of those experiences where your instinct and your anxiety have an argument about which is processing this information accurately. I let anxiety win and moved on. After all, the other actors (some of whom I had coached before and established a trusting relationship with) were open and eager and participatory. So, I figured it was "all in my head."

Rehearsals continued, and I coached individuals in a breakout room separate from the rehearsal room. One by one, the stage manager sent actors in, and our sessions felt productive and playful. Late in the day, the stage manager came to the door and said, "Ellis is not in the right headspace for a session today." I was curious, but since I was also tired, I thought: *Ok. They're working on some emotionally challenging material and may not want to disrupt that to do a dialect session, or maybe they're too tired, or whatever the reason, I'm sure it has nothing to do with me.*

"No problem. We'll work another time." I said with a smile.

But we didn't. I never had a private session with them, and once we began running the show on the actual stage, Sidney and I were talking about a sound Ellis was making that was placing the accent in a different time and place than the character (and the other characters) lived. I confessed to Sidney that I hadn't had a coaching session with Ellis yet. "Yeah, that's not going to happen," Sidney said. And then it hit me. A download of information, faster than regular thought, bypassing the anxious mind completely, shooting straight down to the wisdom of the gut.

"It's because I'm white, isn't it" I said, already knowing the answer.

Sidney looked at me gently and said quietly, "Yes."

"Does anyone else in the cast feel this way?"

"No. Not at all," they quickly answered while shaking their head. "I would tell you."

I trusted that.

Then Sidney shared with me what I needed to know about Ellis's theatrical speech training. Details were kept private, and only general themes were shared, but what I learned then, and since then, was that Ellis's was not an isolated experience.

I returned home that evening with a heavy heart for the harm that had been done to this actor. Although I had experienced harm in my own education, I hadn't had *their* experience. As much as I wanted to have a conversation with them to learn more, this wasn't about what I wanted. It was about honoring Ellis's choice.

Sidney asked me for Ellis's notes and said they would relay them. The rest of the cast continued to work with me as they had been, and soon it was opening night.

Ellis's work was remarkable. I watched their performance, felt their words, and even when I heard the speech sound that still popped out from the world of the play, it just didn't matter anymore. I stopped listening as a dialect coach and started listening as a human.

At the opening night reception, I shared celebratory hugs with each cast member and designer. Glasses of champagne clinked, pictures were taken, and there was so much joy.

I saw Ellis across the lobby, but I wasn't sure if they would welcome my approach. A colleague who accompanied me that evening, said as I stood immobile, "Oh girl, just go over there and say 'Congratulations!'" So, I did.

I walked up to them and since my Italian blood makes my hands move as I speak, my right hand extended with my voice. I was surprised that Ellis took that hand in their hands and held it. I told them how moved I was by the performance while touching my heart with my other hand. Ellis said nothing, just leaned over and kissed me on the cheek. We held eye contact, I spoke more specifically of their work, and they gave me one more quick peck on the cheek before we parted. There were no more words needed.

I teared up a little on the way home. Dumfounded by what had happened, but also touched by what felt like the beginnings of healing. At first, I thought, *maybe they didn't remember me... maybe they thought I was just some nice white lady who saw the show?* I couldn't wrap my head around why an actor who wouldn't even look at me, wouldn't meet with me, would share a tender moment with me... As much as I couldn't intellectualize this, it felt like acceptance with a loving boundary.

Then came 2020. George Floyd was murdered, Black Lives Matter was in motion, and we were isolated from each other in a pandemic paralysis. Yet there was work to do. I studied antiracist pedagogy, listened to students of color, and attended a webinar comprised of white dialect coaches to discuss what we can do to create necessary and lasting change. I learned helpful best practices when working with casts of color and added a coursebook to my academic voice and speech class which was more inclusive, decentered whiteness, and abandoned past precedents of "standard speech." I listened to stories of how black students of mine had been told their "speech was lazy" and how they felt they had to tirelessly code-switch to "sound white" as to be accepted by white people.

Did my defenses ever come up? Of course. I want only to be honest with you, and if I'm not honest about the ugly pieces and parts, then I'm not doing the work. I lived with questions like, "Is it necessary for coach and actor to be of the same race?" and "Do sounds belong to any specific group or individual?" You may have noticed I've kept names and pronouns nonbinary, so perhaps there is an opportunity to move away from binary answers of "yes/no" to these questions as well…

After a year of "Zoom Plays," 2021's triumphant return to live theater was a welcomed return indeed. And I emitted a sound of glee when there in my inbox was a coaching request from Sidney to return to the theater where we were last together with another story by the same playwright. Everything I learned from our previous show and from 2020 was there before me. I called Sidney before I typed anything in reply.

We talked, and Sidney said they already knew what I was going to say. They assured me that they did want me, specifically, to coach, that they had given it a lot of consideration, and would I accept? I thought about turning down the gig and recommending they use a coach of color, but then it occurred to me that it was not my responsibility to tell a black director what was best for their project. Were I being asked by a white director, I would strongly recommend they hire a coach of color because having both a white director and a white dialect coach for black stories and voices feels egregiously wrong. But after listening to Sidney, I accepted and offered actions I could take to effect change.

I got to work. The first rehearsal was a few months away, and I wanted to do a lot of things differently. I consulted other dialect coaches for best practices that were non-performative, but honest and hopefully, healing. This time, before the research, sound samples, and sound analysis, my dialect packet for the cast began with "Statements of Consciousness and Care." I am grateful to Adi Cabral, Associate Professor of Voice and Movement at the University of Nevada, Reno, for invaluable guidance and some of the language below. These statements were not to be read aloud by me, as I felt that would be performative. Instead, it was the first slide of my presentation:

I am aware that I am a white dialect coach, describing the speech sounds of black voices.

I am not the expert on this experience, and I have deferred to resources of native speakers for support.

I am not the gatekeeper of these voices. I am a researcher who has curated resources for you. I have not lived this experience but can refer you to coaches with first-hand knowledge to supplement our work if necessary.

The following descriptions of sounds are technical, linguistic, descriptions, rather than prescriptions of how you should speak, according to me. They are options for you as you find your character's voice. I am here to support you, and to assist you with the physical realization of any sound you may (or may not) need.

I treat sounds with respect and care.

Should you feel unsupported in any way, or should you experience any harm from our work, please communicate with me.

I will listen without any denial of your experience.

My phone rang, and it was Sidney.

"I wanted to tell you that we have a cast. There are some folks you've coached before – they're excited to work with you again – and I'm also casting Ellis, so maybe we can talk about that."

Reader, please pause for a minute with me here. Because when I heard that, I was in complete and humble awe of how the Universe works. I hope you see it too.

I told Sidney that I would like to make sure Ellis is ok with me coaching the show. I proposed a conversation between the three of us before the first rehearsal if Ellis was open to that. Sidney said they would reach out to them and circle back to me. I continued with my research.

Sidney and I met over Zoom to review my materials, but first we discussed Ellis, with whom Sidney had had an individual conversation. They said that Ellis seemed to be in a very different place, was enthused that I was joining the production team, didn't seem to have any negative feelings about it, and kept saying that they were excited to see "what the *group* would come up with, and what the *group* would do." Sidney made a point that the word "group" was emphasized.

Group. "*What the group will come up with.*" Of course! The *group* should come up with how they speak because it is with each other they speak the most. I still researched sound samples and analyzed those samples, but Ellis's words inspired me to go further.

The first rehearsal came, and it was an actual, physical room filled with reunions, hugs, masked smiles, and laughter. I saw Ellis. We fist bumped, pandemic style. I could see their eyes were smiling.

The cast began the table read, and I'll take a moment to say that one of the sweetest sounds to hear is the sound of actors lifting the words off the page and filling the air with their voices—especially when you have been without the vibration of live voices for a year and a half.

A few nights later, I returned to give my dialect presentation. I gave a moment for the cast to read the Statements. No one had a response, so before moving on to the samples and analysis, we had a conversation about where we were each from, where we had lived, and what language or accent influences were there throughout our lives. What were our speech stories?

We learned that many of the cast had been born and spent part of their youth in the same area as each other. "I didn't know you were from____!" was heard a lot. Many of us had worked together before and yet had no idea where we were all from, and how we ended up in California. People shared where their family members were from, if they spoke additional languages, how moving from here to there influenced their speech, and then this crucial part of the stories: "When I was at [insert University/Conservatory here] they beat my accent outta me." "I had to get rid of…" "It's hard for me to unlearn…" and so on, and yes, much of this is verbatim.

We discussed how their characters had migrated from one area of the United States to another, and although they would have shared sounds, what sounds might be unique to them? If two characters spent more time talking to each other, and/or were family members, would they share more sounds than with other characters? I proposed to the cast that this could be their collaborative decision rather than one dictated by me. For example, there were speakers who pronounced "window" as /WIN-doh/ and /WIN-duh/. Both were appropriate to the time and place, so this was a creative choice to be made by *the group*.

I shared resources and guided them through analysis, being sure to model isolated sounds but not the speech in its entirety, and then I turned it over to them. They discussed what sounds they've heard older family members use from that region, and which characters might speak those sounds. They asked each other questions, and Ellis was engaged. Ellis was playing a character who would, at specific moments, target sounds unique from the others—something they were already exploring in the table read. Sidney and I had discussed a much more "hands off" approach with Ellis, so when Ellis's character came up, I said, "and I have resources for you if you want or need them." "Oh, I know you do!" Ellis said cheerfully.

We finished the dialect work for the evening, and Sidney and I discussed how noticeably different Ellis's energy was this time. I ran into some of the cast in the stairwell as I was headed home, and they were taking their breaks. Lots of hugs and then a look exchanged with Ellis. They approached me, gave me a huge hug, and thanked me for coming.

I never had one private session with Ellis during the rest of the rehearsal process. That had not changed. Some cast members noticed this and even inquired about it, but since there were other parts of Ellis's process that were unique, they didn't push the topic for long. We focused on supporting them instead.

On a drive home, I thought about equity and equality. Ellis was given the same information and opportunity as everyone else in the cast, and, they had specific needs of space and autonomy. Sidney relayed any notes I had to Ellis, yet other cast members would call me while I was driving on the freeway to double-check a pronunciation.

The show opened to repeated standing ovations and rave reviews. I was thrilled for the cast, and honored and humbled to have been part of the process. Moreso, I was grateful for the lesson, and for more than one opportunity to learn it.

Resources:

For inclusive, skills-based, speech training, please visit Knight-Thompson Speechwork: www.ktspeechwork.org

Questions for Meditation:
1. What is your speech story?
2. What prejudices and preferences might you have regarding speech?
3. Did you or do you have models for "good speech?" and what does "good speech" mean to you?

Figure 25.1 A mountain. (Credit: Andrea Odinov.)

Dearest Teacher,

The students you have before you are the students you need at this time.

Always with Love,

The Universe

Chapter 26
There's Always One

Over the years of teaching at various institutions, conservatories, and studios, I've often said with a sigh, "There's always one." There's always that *one* student who triggers me or, worse, affects the group dynamic so negatively that if they are not in attendance one day, I can feel the energy in the room shift. I feel this today as deeply as I did in my earliest days of teaching. But what I didn't know then that I do know now is that this "one" is the student who came to teach me about myself.

I've met these student-teachers in various forms; below is a sampling. As you read this partial list of potentials, notice if anything comes up for you: an image, a breath, or a sensation…

The one who is always late, and sometimes, loudly late. Makes every noise possible until seated.
The one who asks questions before you've completed a sentence.
The one who answers all the questions before anyone else.
The one who won't engage with you or with classmates.
The one who will engage, with their phone. A lot.
The one who is an expert because they already learned everything from their acting coach.

The one who pulls focus.
The one with all the jokes.
The one with all the charm.
The one who doesn't know why they're there and/or doesn't want to be there.
The one who reminds you of someone you don't like.
The one who reminds you of yourself.

What could each one of these student-teachers teach you? Not just about your pedagogy, but about *you*?

Confession: I see versions of my former student self in at least five of the above forms.

Know what else? Sometimes they come back. Yes, that student that you experienced in such a way that you breathed a deep sigh of relief once the class was completed—will show up again. Maybe it will literally be the same student or a new student who exhibits the behavior or shares the personality that caused you to tighten. If it was the one who didn't want to be there, you might wonder how they found their way into your classroom again. Perhaps they had to, according to schedule or major requirements, but a more exciting possibility to meditate on is that *now there is an opportunity for a different relationship: with them and with yourself.*

The Opportunity

One of my "one's" showed up again, two and a half years after my first class with them. The initial experience wasn't a nightmare; it just wasn't one I cared to repeat. The student was consistently late, brought a frenetic, disruptive energy into the space, and did not wish to work with or even be physically near anyone. In the middle of more than one lesson, the student would release a loud, exacerbated sigh, which normally I welcome in a voice class—to give voice to one's experience—but this sigh pulled my focus away from my instruction, and I perceived it as a huge "I'm bored as hell." This was a new class I was teaching, and I couldn't help but project upon that sigh my insecurity about whether the course was any good. Mid-semester, the student did not do as well as they hoped on a midterm assessment and approached me to desperately seek extra credit to make up for their low score. I wrote them a long, detailed email, outlined options, assessed their current grade, and explained how I would support them. There was no response, but the sighs and disengagement continued.

In hindsight, there were missed opportunities on my end. I did not reach out to this student to check in or inquire if there were ways in which I could better support them aside from honoring their need for physical distance in class and offering options to improve their grade. I was distracted that semester. As I mentioned, it was the first semester of a new class I was teaching, which is usually clunky, as well as my first semester as a full-time professor, which also felt clunky. So, my energy, which is normally entirely focused on my students, was scattered.

Course evaluations are anonymous. There is no way to know who-wrote-what and that is a precious protection of privacy. But one student out of that very small class that for the most part reviewed both the course and me positively gave me horrendously low scores, the likes of which I hadn't seen in over a decade of teaching. And in the area for comments regarding the course itself were words I'd never read before on any of my evaluations:

"This shit sucks."

I will never know who felt that way, of course, but I immediately suspected it was "the one." I think I also just decided it was them, based upon nothing but my anxiety and shame. I felt confusion and failure, recalled that everyone, including, and especially "the one" bid me a cheerful "Thank You!" and good-bye at the end of each class. No one seemed *that* miserable. I felt sucker punched. I never wanted to teach that student again, even if they weren't the one who wrote those words. Not an enlightened or even mature thought, I admit. My defenses: up, my armor: on.

Two and a half years later, there they were on my roster, and when I saw their name, I made a sound that I can't phonetically transcribe. They enrolled this time in a class that I feared they would label "More Sucky Shit" a logical next level of suckitude from the previous introductory course. My mind raced through scenarios of how they were going to react to what can be a very intense class for the willing, let alone the very guarded. I breathed. Barely.

That semester in the more advanced class, they were still "them", but something had changed, in both of us. My energy was more focused, and since presence is a component of my curriculum, I made a conscious decision to be here now with this student, to teach the student in front of me, and not to react to whom I perceived them to be in the past. I noticed they were more engaged, willing, and open than before, even though this was during the Covid Pandemic, and we were still online in our Zoom rectangles. Perhaps online learning alleviated the discomfort of physical proximity to classmates and allowed more space for the student's growth.

At one point in the semester, they began to experience several traumatic personal events, in addition to the trauma we all were already undergoing during 2020 through 2021. I immediately reached out this time, and this reach was met with their reach. They confided in me about what they were trying to manage, and it was not easy, everyday stuff. This information shed light on past behavior, and I began to understand more about them. I asked if they had both University and professional support, which they did, and we talked about how we could integrate the coursework with what was occurring in their life. One day, I received a heartfelt email about how much my initial inquiry meant to them, and the communication grew and improved between us. I learned to let this student be who they were, and that who they were had nothing to do with me. They mostly needed to work asynchronously for a better part of the semester, and they did, indeed, work. Their needs were different from my other students', and I learned more about how equity is not "special treatment" and even if it were, some students need that too.

At the end of the semester, we met (virtually) to discuss their grade, what they learned, and their challenges, and I remarked about how much they had grown since that first class two and a half years ago. They said, "I never want to be my 19 yr. old self again." I laughed, and said, "Neither do I."

At the end of the conversation, we shared a breath, as this was their final semester of college and graduation was next. In-person graduation had been postponed until the end of summer, and it was to be held in a large stadium as a combined graduation ceremony for both the classes of 2020 and 2021 instead of our usual intimate ceremony on campus.

They said, "I want to find all of the people who are important to me in that giant stadium, and you're one of them, so I hope I can find you and take a picture of us." I said, "Absolutely" with a heartfelt smile, and we ended our meeting.

I wept with gratitude for this second chance. This chance to be more observant, more present, and more active in checking in with my students, as well as the chance to forgive my former self for not having done so the first time this student was in my class. I wept at the beauty of growth, maturity, and a sense of completion. I wept with joy and absolute wonder at how this student showed up again and that what I initially feared, ultimately felt so freeing.

I think I learned the lesson, but we'll see because this student will show up again in a different form.

The good news is, I'll be in a different form as well, and will welcome each variation of "the one" as:

The one who gives you the gift of growth.

Questions for Meditation:
1. If you dread "the one" coming into your class... why?
2. What, exactly, are you dreading? Do they introduce you to and/or challenge your assumptions, judgments, patience, forgiveness, understanding, or curiosity?
3. Are they reflecting unreconciled aspects of your former student self?
4. Is the impulse to "correct their behavior" a way to go back in time and correct yours?

Chapter 27
There's More than Meets the Ear

I'm going to call her "Stella," the Italian word for "star," for her light could shine so brightly when it wasn't clouded by protection, judgment, and fear.

Stella arrived at my voice class with a forced smile—a smile that was for everyone else but her. She smiled to be liked, as many of us wish to be, especially on our first day at a new school. The tension from the effort of maintaining this smile—regardless of whether she truly felt like smiling—spread from her cheeks to her tongue to her throat to her voice. I heard other students and teachers refer to her voice as a "baby voice," perceived as "high-pitched," "tight," and "cute." Some thought she *was* cute, others felt they couldn't take her seriously. Some found her sound annoying, and I'll admit that I shared some of those thoughts when I first heard her, as well. Regardless of how she was perceived, that was the voice that her listeners were accustomed to. She told me that she didn't particularly like her voice, but she didn't know what to do about it.

An exceptional student, she fully committed to a journey of self-discovery and expression. During one class, as I walked around the room to observe my students, Stella's voice stopped me in my tracks. I heard her, and I mean *her*. Her voice was open, unbridled, and resonant with sound and sensation I hadn't heard from her before. She moved out of the dynamic effort she was in, sat up, and looked at me, her eyes wet.

"*Did you feel that?*" I asked.

"*Yes*," she managed to say, as her voice closed back up with the smile.

"*That's a new depth of you*," I told her lovingly.

She nodded, and I let her be to sit with that sensation.

Following that class, she sought private sessions with me. We worked together for weeks, in a sound-proof room, where she didn't have to worry about anyone hearing her fall apart and put herself back together again. As we worked, I suggested she only smile if she authentically felt the impulse. Her face softened in relief. We continued to explore layers of tension release and help her body relearn what it intuitively knew how to do, which is breathe and express itself. Tears flowed as her body's protective armor melted, making room for joy as she discovered aspects of herself that she hadn't yet experienced. Her courage was remarkable.

Stella did not smile when she said that her mother told her she "wasn't pretty enough to be an actress." But as her work progressed, and she *felt* her voice from a much deeper place within, she placed her hand upon her center, not her face, and said, "*When I feel my voice here, I feel like a woman. I feel beautiful.*" The clouds parted, and she beamed.

She desperately wanted to share this with the world, but she was afraid. She was afraid that people would think she was trying to sound like someone else. She was afraid that she would be unrecognizable. Would she still be liked if she didn't wear a smile on her face despite the depression she struggled with her entire time at school? *(I'm very mindful of my lane as a teacher and am careful not to cross over into a therapist's. So, as I helped her with the physical and energetic aspects, I made sure that she had appropriate support for the emotional and psychological.)*

Her fear was not unreasonable. Her first attempt to reveal the depth of her voice was met by her roommate with an abrasive, "*Why are you talking like that?!*" She felt judged and defeated. She wasn't trying to play a role. She was trying to encourage and share *her* voice—the voice that had been hiding in her body and was afraid to come out for fear of reactions just like her roommate's.

This question: "Why are you talking like that?" is problematic because the "that" to which they are referring might be the result of a long, emotional process, requiring the speaker to give up a trusted pattern of behavior that felt comfortable, reliable, and safe. An integrated voice reveals one's humanity, without guards, blocks, or masks. It is a vibrational expression of what a person is experiencing. It is not always polite, perfect, or pretty. It can make others uncomfortable.

To be fair, it's not as though the question itself is inherently offensive, it's more the tone the inquirer chooses, which may well be rooted in curiosity. They might be thinking, *you suddenly sound different—why?* But for the person who is so delicately, and often painfully, exposing their voice to the world, it can trigger self-consciousness or self-doubt, and as a result, the armor activates and the voice retreats inside for protection... Stella's voice was walking a tightrope of habit when what it wanted to do was fly through the air with the greatest of ease...

Over the next three years, I observed Stella struggle with how much she was willing to reveal to others when she was not performing. What I didn't do was follow her around and remind her of what we'd worked on. Students learn on their own timetables, and each body most certainly has its own timetable, independent of what schedule the mind would prefer. There are physical, emotional, and psychological aspects to the voice, and integrating the three does not happen overnight or even over the course of a semester. She took one other class with me and requested vocal coaching for her role in a department production. I enjoyed how much more of her voice she was sharing and stepped back with compassion when she was protecting. What I wanted her to learn was that we do need to protect at times. That's ok. Our armor can be a necessary function of the body to limit sensation and not overcharge the nervous system. That said, the project is about awareness and choice. Awareness of one's habitual armor and whether it is necessary in the present moment.

Stella shed light on how we can choose to respond when a voice we hear brings up a negative reaction. We can recoil, judge, and try to change a voice to suit our ears, or we can respond with an open heart, a curious mind, and a soft space for that voice to tell its story.

Throughout my years of teaching, I've met more than one "Stella." On the first day of each voice class, I begin with a blind poll. With eyes closed, students are prompted to raise their hand if their answers to the following feel like a yes:

1. Do you like your voice?
2. Has your voice ever been criticized?

I have been taking this poll two to three times a year for almost 15 years and have yet to meet a class where everyone raises their hand for number one or does not raise their hands for number two.

So now, I'll ask you:

1. Do you like your voice?
2. Has your voice ever been criticized?
3. Has either affected how you communicate with others, either professionally or personally?

Chapter 28
Lessons from My Recent Role as a Student

Beyond the lessons your students will teach you, there are lessons to be gained from being a student—specifically, in the discipline you teach. And the longer it's been since you were a student, the more valuable experiences like this become.

Recently, I took a week-long course in a particular method of speech training. Although I am familiar with and teach aspects of this methodology, it has been quite some time since I studied the foundations for this work, so it felt right to revisit both the information and the experience of receiving that information.

I'll begin by noting that the two teachers were excellent: both with a skillset and pedagogy that is remarkable and inspirational. They co-taught with expertise, humility, patience, presence, compassion, creativity, humor, respect for the work, each other, and the students. Students were comprised of mostly university, college, or conservatory teachers, private practitioners, and a few performers. I spend a moment honoring these teachers because I am now aware of something I wasn't decades ago: the "Things" that came up for me during the course, which could have been perceived as negative, were created by *me*, and not a product of their pedagogy. This isn't always the case, as there certainly are teachers who, despite their best intentions, do harm by way of their methods, or even their choice of words. This was not one of those cases.

It surprised me most that these "Things" came up at all! I assumed that being halfway through my life, having a career filled with positive reviews, and maintaining a daily practice of mindfulness meditation, I would have evolved *beyond* feelings of insecurity, comparison and shame, discomfort, resistance, or the need for validation. Evidently not. The evolution I have achieved is in the awareness of these feelings and in my ability to reflect on them. Since I regularly facilitate my students through their own "Things," which may or may not resemble mine, I found it curious that mine still arose. They affected me, regardless of my outstanding teachers and the brave, safe space they created.

So here are the "Things," in no particular order:

(…or are they?)

> Peoples' stories are so interesting.
> What will I say when the introduction circle stops at me?
> Learning is fun!
> Learning is uncomfortable…
> Oh shit, I've been doing that one thing, um, wrong. And that other thing. That was wrong too… Why didn't I know it was wrong?

Hurray! I knew that thing! I was right! See?!
I can't do this other thing.
I just did it!
I want to volunteer in the game!
Have I been volunteering too much?
I'm going to be open, and vulnerable, and say this thing….
I'm talking too much.
My back hurts in this chair.
These teachers are amazing! I wish I could teach that way.
A-ha!
Oops.
Ouch.
This is fascinating….
My mind is wandering….

WAIT—WE HAVE TO DO MONOLOGUES?!?

I'm not doing it.
I'm going to do it.
Why don't I want to do it? Lean into the discomfort. Very curious about my resistance.
Holy heart rate and sweating…DISCOMFORT.
I did it! Victory!
…Was it good?
Let it go.
This space feels incredibly safe. I love the people I'm studying with.
My brain just folded in half.
I'm so inspired! I can't stop smiling, and my heart feels so open…

I'm so tired.
I'm irritable.

I still have so many questions.

Questions for Meditation:
1. Did judgments come up for you as you read the things? If the things you just read were expressed by your student (either spoken or perhaps journaled), what might come up for you?
2. Can you relate to any of them? As a student? As a teacher? As an artist?
3. Which of these things could potentially come up for a student, and what might the indicators be?

Chapter 29
When Death Comes

I missed it. She was the most outgoing, dedicated, and joyful student.

Complete and utter shock at opening the university email: "It is with sad somethingorother that…" Her name. Jaw drop. Keen.

The Day After:

Arrive to campus. Hugs. Are you okay? Crying and holding.

They all knew. Lesson plan pivot.

"No books. We're not doing any of that today."

We sit in a circle. They look to me for answers. They look to the floor for grounding. They just saw her the other day… social media had no hints, until it was deleted, and she was gone.

One student breaks the silence with, "Can I go?" I nod, and out the door they go to process alone. Different needs. A need to continue and a need to stop. A need to talk and a need to sit in silence.

The Days After:

We sit in our usual circle, but we are no longer 14.

"Do you want to include her chair?"

Let's leave a chair to the side, they decide.

How to proceed?

I offer that both feelings can exist: we can remember, honor, grieve, miss her terribly…and we can still have fun. We can still laugh, as we did, as she did, and remind ourselves that we are still living.

We create a ritual. LED votive candles for each student to "light" with thoughts of her. Each candle is placed on her chair, outside the circle but still in the space. The candles remain lit for the length of each class.

The Years After:

Her picture adorns my office. I have students talk to her beautiful face when they practice their monologues during coaching sessions. I think of her every year, on the anniversary of her passing. And I check in with my students more—especially the outgoing, dedicated, and joyful ones with amazing social media profiles.

I can't prepare for nor predict when it will come. All I feel I can do is remain as present as possible with my students so that when it comes, I can respond in a way that feels helpful, hopeful, and healing.

Meditation Practice:
Let each reminder of your mortality,
deepen your gratitude for life:
this moment
here now always.

Chapter 30
Holding Space

This is a space and an opportunity for a community knowledge exchange. Is there a lesson from one of your students that you'd like to process? Here is a template to construct your own lesson from your students to discuss with your classmates, trusted colleagues, or the authors! To honor your students' privacy, it's a good idea to remove any of their personally identifiable information. #lessonsfromourstudents @lessonsfromourstudents

Describe the inciting incident or presenting problem:

Establish the given circumstances and relationships, the heart of your inquiry.

Hover in the unknown:

What questions come up for you? What feelings or sensations do you notice?

Hunker for discernment:

What are possible courses of action? Is there a mantra or meditation practice from the book to explore? What wisdom arises in your breath, body, and being?

Lessons from My Co-Author

"Do you want to write a book with me?" Stacey asked.

I couldn't answer. Partly because I had just taken a bite of dining hall food, and partly because I couldn't believe the question. The only writing of mine that Stacey had read was my "Office Hours" sign that hung outside my door, so, why me? I also thought *why me* because when someone who was once very important to me said that I "couldn't put two sentences together," and that "my stories were boring," I believed it.

"What kind of book?" I mumbled through what I believed at the time to be meat.

As she described her idea, I felt that feeling I get when I know to say yes. It was exactly the book I wanted to write. I had been brimming with student stories I wanted to tell for years but was too afraid. And I was still afraid, but it felt like since we were both taking a risk, why not lean into that fear and see where it could lead?

Creating with Stacey was a transformative experience. She soon dispelled those beliefs I held, and as I wrote, the limiting stories I told myself regarding my abilities were rewritten by her unfailing support. I was and am inspired by Stacey's ability to listen, collaborate, honor an individual's strengths and contributions, respect the other's time and bandwidth, and give kind, constructive feedback that empowers and inspires. We worked in each other's offices, in each other's homes, and during pandemic isolation, we Facetimed and read our writing to each other over the phone. Eventually, we began to meet in the mountains to have moving conversations while on hikes, followed by food. Lots of food. This process with Stacey has fed both my belly and my soul.

Thank you, dearest colleague and friend, for inviting me on this walk of faith, this walk of wisdom, and this walk of wonder. Thank you for walking alongside me the entire time.

Figure C.1 Learning alongside each other. (Credit: Andrea Odinov.)

As you may have discerned through reading this book, Andrea is an extraordinary teacher. I knew this in the first week that we met. I heard it in the way she spoke of her students with deep respect, lovingkindness, and enthusiasm for their development. I felt it from my office across the hall (aka Vibration Alley), where she would vocally coach our actors and elicit in their instruments unprecedented power, freedom, and expressivity. The students would often emerge from those sessions with shining eyes, beaming with newfound confidence. In Andrea's wholehearted presence, her students became more of themselves. And while she is humble about her pedagogical prowess, I knew that she had much to teach her colleagues as well.

For the last five years, we have debriefed after countless classes and faculty meetings. Along the way, we launched a graduate program, survived pandemic pedagogy, and worked on countless productions. Our triumphs and (many) tribulations would become the basis of this book. Through Andrea's patience and encouragement, I eventually found my voice as a first-time author. And for her Marble Jar Friendship, brilliance, and inspiration, I will always be grateful.

Bibliography

Anderson, Michael. *Master Class in Drama Education: Transforming Teaching and Learning*. United Kingdom, Bloomsbury Academic, 2011.

"Appreciation, Apology, Aha." Facing History and Ourselves, 30 June 2021. https://www.facinghistory.org/resource-library/appreciation-apology-aha

Arvidson, P. Sven. *Teaching Nonmajors: Advice for Liberal Arts Professors*. United States, State University of New York Press, 2008.

Barron, Nancy G., et al. *Social Change in Diverse Teaching Contexts: Touchy Subjects and Routine Practices*. Austria, Peter Lang, 2006.

Brackett, Marc A. *Permission to Feel: Unlocking the Power of Emotions to Help Our Kids, Ourselves, and Our Society Thrive*. United States, Celadon Books, 2019.

Brown, Brené. *Daring Greatly: How the Courage to Be Vulnerable Transforms the Way We Live, Love, Parent, and Lead*. United Kingdom, Penguin Books Limited, 2013.

Chapman, Diana. "Whole Body Yes." The Conscious Leadership Group, 2021. https://conscious.is/concepts/leading-and-living-from-your-whole-body-yes

"Chicago Theatre Standards." Not in Our House: Chicago Theatre Community, 2017. https://notinourhouseorg.wordpress.com/

Chödrön, Pema. *No Time to Lose: A Timely Guide to the Way of the Bodhisattva*. United States, Shambhala Publications, 2005.

Chödrön, Pema. *Start Where You Are: How to Accept Yourself and Others*. United States, Element, 2005.

Chödrön, Pema. *The Places That Scare You: A Guide to Fearlessness in Difficult Times*. United States, Shambhala, 2007.

Chun, Malcolm Naea. *Ho'oponopono: Traditional Ways of Healing to Make Things Right Again*. United States, Curriculum Research & Development Group, University of Hawaii, 2006.

"Community Guidelines and Transformative Justice." Pedagogy and Theatre of the Oppressed Conference Guide, 2019. https://ptoweb.org/wp-content/uploads/2019/06/PTO2019-Guide-COMPLETE-v5-Digital.pdf

Congreve, William, and Roberts, David. *The Way of the World*. Bloomsbury Methuen Drama, 2020.

Crozier, Rebecca. "F.A.I.L.—a Meditation on the Suckiness of Failing." The Modern Meditator, 11 June 2021. https://themodernmeditator.com.au/fail/

Cruz, M. Colleen. *Risk. Fail. Rise: A Teacher's Guide to Learning from Mistakes*. United States, Heinemann, 2020.

Dahl, Roald. *Matilda*. United States, Penguin Young Readers, 2020.

Delpit, Lisa. *Teaching When the World Is on Fire: Authentic Classroom Advice, from Climate Justice to Black Lives Matter*. United States, New Press, 2021.

Estill, Jo, et al. *The Estill Voice Model*. United States, Estill Voice International, LLC, 2017.

Gallagher, Kathleen. *Why Theatre Matters: Urban Youth, Engagement, and a Pedagogy of the Real*. Canada, University of Toronto Press, 2014.

Geest, Kaatje de, et al. *Why Theatre?* Berlin, NTGent, 2020.

Hobbs, Lorraine, et al. *Teaching Self-Compassion to Teens*. United States, Guilford Publications, 2022.

Holland, Braden. Interview. Conducted by Stacey Cabaj, 2022.

Homan, Sidney. *Why the Theatre: In Personal Essays, College Teachers, Actors, Directors, and Playwrights Tell Why the Theatre Is So Vital to Them*. United States, Routledge, 2021.

Johncock, Philip Duane. "Limbo & Authentic Yes' and No's." Hendricks Institute, 2007. https://hendricks.com/limbo-authentic-yes-and-nos/

Katschke, Judy. *The Magic School Bus Rides Again: Sink or Swim*. United States, Scholastic, 2018.

Klotz-Guest, Kathy. "Six Steps to Turn Jargon-Monoxide into Human Speak That Connects." Convince & Convert, 8 July 2014. https://www.convinceandconvert.com/content-marketing/six-steps-to-turn-jargon-monoxide-into-human-speak-that-connects/

Lahey, Jessica. "Should Teachers Be Allowed to Touch Students?" The Atlantic, Atlantic Media Company, 31 May 2018. https://www.theatlantic.com/education/archive/2015/01/the-benefits-of-touch/384706/

Lang, K.D. "Constant Craving." Spotify. https://open.spotify.com/track/0wCrg1LhgPcGMw51qqpI6k

McMahon, Edwin M., and Campbell, Peter A. *Please Touch*. United States, Sheed and Ward, 1969.

"Mental Health First Aid USA." Mental Health First Aid, 3 Nov. 2022. https://www.mentalhealthfirstaid.org/

Mintz, Steven. "Combating the Commodification of Higher Education: Inside Higher Ed." Inside Higher Ed, 6 June 2020. https://www.insidehighered.com/blogs/higher-ed-gamma/combating-commodification-higher-education

Montgomery, Lucy Maude. *Illustrated Green Gables: Anne of Green Gables*. United States, Sea Wolf Press, 2020.

Nachmanovitch, Stephen. *The Art of Is: Improvising as a Way of Life*. United States, New World Library, 2019.

Nagoski, Emily, and Nagoski, Amelia. *Burnout: The Secret to Unlocking the Stress Cycle*. United States, Random House Publishing Group, 2019.

Ostaseski, Frank. "How You Can Help." Metta Meditation, 2011. https://www.mettainstitute.org/mettameditation.html

Pace, Chelsea, and Rikard, Laura. *Staging Sex: Best Practices, Tools, and Techniques for Theatrical Intimacy*. United States, Routledge, 2020.

Palmer, Parker J., et al. *The Heart of Higher Education: A Call to Renewal*. Germany, Wiley, 2010.

Pearson, Andrew. "Returning to Theatre with Enthusiastic Consent." HowlRound Theatre Commons, 11 May 2021. https://howlround.com/returning-theatre-enthusiastic-consent

Perone, Kim. "Learn to Meditate." Center4C, 24 Sept. 2019. https://www.center4c.com/learn-to-meditate/

Pierson, Rita F. "Every Kid Needs a Champion." *TED Talk*, 2013. https://www.ted.com/talks/rita_pierson_every_kid_needs_a_champion/transcript

Pressfield, Steven. *The War of Art: Break through the Blocks and Win Your Inner Creative Battles*. United States, Black Irish Entertainment LLC, 2002.

Quesada, Donna. *Buddha in the Classroom*. United States, Skyhorse Publishing, 2011.

Ristad, Eloise. *A Soprano on Her Head: Right-Side-up Reflections on Life and Other Performances*. United States, Real People Press, 2002.

Rodenburg, Patsy. "Why I Do Theater." *Patsy Rodenburg: Why I Do Theater | TED Talk*. https://www.ted.com/talks/patsy_rodenburg_why_i_do_theater

Rome, Chip, and Dillard, Zoë. *Real-World Theatre Education: A Teacher's Guide to Growing a Theatre Education Program*. United States, Educational Stages, 2015.

Sajnani, Nisha. "A Drama Therapist's Perspective on Teaching Theatre in Times of Crisis." HowlRound Theatre Commons, 21 July 2020. https://howlround.com/drama-therapists-perspective-teaching-theatre-times-crisis

Sajnani, Nisha, and Johnson, David Read. *Trauma-informed Drama Therapy: Transforming Clinics, Classrooms, and Communities*. United States, Charles C. Thomas, Publisher, Limited, 2014.

Scribner, Megan, and Intrator, Sam M. *Teaching with Fire: Poetry That Sustains the Courage to Teach*. United Kingdom, Wiley, 2003.

Scribner, Megan, and Palmer, Parker J. *The Courage to Teach Guide for Reflection and Renewal*. United Kingdom, Wiley, 2007.

Scrivener, Jim. *MBT Learning Teaching*. 3rd ed., United States, MacMillan ELT, 2011.

Shawyer, Susanne, and Shively, Kim. "Education in Theatrical Intimacy as Ethical Practice for University Theatre." Journal of Dramatic Theory and Criticism, vol. 34 no. 1, 2019, p. 87–104. Project MUSE, doi:10.1353/dtc.2019.0025

Shute, Scott. *The Full Body Yes: Change Your Work and Your World from the Inside Out*. United States, Page Two Books, 2021.

Smith, Lauri. "The Power of the Hunker." *Voice Matters*, 27 Sept. 2020. https://voice-matters.com/the-power-of-the-hunker

Smyth, Cliff. "Attunement through the Body." Feldenkrais Center for Movement and Awareness, 2011. https://www.feldenkraissf.com/attunement-through-the-body

Spalding, Dan. *How to Teach Adults: Plan Your Class, Teach Your Students, Change the World, Expanded Edition*. Germany, Wiley, 2014.

Stutland, Erin. *Mantras in Motion: Manifesting What You Want through Mindful Movement*. United States, Hay House, 2020.

Tharp, Twyla. *The Collaborative Habit: Life Lessons for Working Together*. United Kingdom, Simon & Schuster, 2009.

Walker, Pete. *Complex PTSD: From Surviving to Thriving: A Guide and Map for Recovering from Childhood Trauma.* United States, Azure Coyote, 2013.

Wangh, Stephen. *An Acrobat of the Heart: A Physical Approach to Acting Inspired by the Work of Jerzy Grotowski.* United Kingdom, Knopf Doubleday Publishing Group, 2000.

World Bank. *The Art of Knowledge Exchange: A Results-Focused Planning Guide for Development Practitioners.* Open Knowledge Repository, 2018.

Worley, Lee. *Coming from Nothing: The Sacred Art of Acting.* United States, Turquoise Dragon Press, 2001.

Yankovic, Al. "Mission Statement." Spotify. https://open.spotify.com/track/6qtiyGOzgHIfIX4wJmit2g?si=5c5c341c0616435e

Index

acting class 35–37, 51, 52
ahimsa (nonviolence) 42
anger 72–73
Anne of Green Gables (Montgomery) 31
anxiety 34–37, 85; dynamic of 13–14; and shame 100
apologies 40–41; mindful and meaningful 41
appreciation 41
attention to students 60–64

believing in students 53
Black Lives Matter 88
bodily autonomy 44
body: armor 107; exploring 59
bodywork 59
breathing-thinking-feeling-reacting 72
breath release work 59

Cabral, Adi 90
check-in exercise 7–8
circle up mashup 7–8
Cole, Joanna 31
communication 101
communicative language teaching framework 9
community: agreement 5–6; knowledge exchange 115
compassion 109

Congreve, William 51
consent x, 43, 44
course: evaluations 99; modules 13–14
COVID-19 pandemic 71, 101
creative hunker 50
creativity 109
cultural memos 11–12
curiosity and enthusiasm 6

Dahl, Roald 32
death 113–114
decision making 19
democratization of knowledge 11–12
dialect work 83, 92
digital story-catching survey 53
diversity 68
dream anger 66
dream-self 66

ecosystem of love 5–6
ego's reaction 60
emotional release 70
encouragement 53
energy: in class room 77–81; shift 77–78
equity 68
Estill Voice Training (EVT®) 43
evaluations 26–27

fail, prepare to 63
fawn response 41
Fitzmaurice Voicework® ix, 59, 61, 70
Floyd, George, murder 88
foreign language acquisition 9
frustration 33

Gallagher, Kathleen 3
Generation Z, teaching 68
grading 24–25; getting a 20; giving a 20; performance-based classes 20–25
graduation ceremony 102
Grotowski-based practices 48
group 91–92

Heuvel, Wendy Vanden 48
Hippocratic Oath 79
holding space for silence 10
hovering 48
human with emotions 74
humility 109
humor 109
hunkering 48–50

impatience 33–34
imposter syndrome 31, 68–69
inclusion practices 68
inner guidance system 46
inspire students 53
instructional touch 43
internal sensations 7

jargon 11–12
jargon-monoxide poisoning 11

kind, being 53
Klotz-Guest, Kathy 11
Knight-Thompson Speechwork® 95

language 11–12
lifelines 6
loving-kindness meditation 34

Matilda (Dahl) 32
meditation 50, 66; loving-kindness 34; mindfulness 110; music 12; somatic 46; walking 56
memorizing text 35
Mental Health First Aid 36
mental rigidity in teaching 69
mind-body-spirit connection 50
mindfulness practices 37
Montgomery, Lucy Maude 31

nature-based lessons 31

online: learning 53, 74, 101; learning tool 13–14; pedagogy 68
outdoor classes 31
Owen, Wilfred 16

patience 109
pedagogical: decision 47; icon 31; risks 69
perennial questions 19
perfect student 64
permission slips 38–39, *39*
personal life problems 77–82
personhood 7
physical culture exercises 31
physical realization of sounds 84
practice of freedom 5
presence 109
present arms 18
present-moment awareness 7
prototypes 31–32

INDEX   125

readings 38
reserve officers' training core (ROTC) cadets 16
resistence in teaching 69
responsiveness 35
risk and failure, culture of 51–52
Rodenburg, Patsy 3

self-assessment report 23
self-congratulatory thought 66
self-evaluation stress 23
self-imposed pressure 13
self-reflection and evaluation 22
Shakespeare Theatre Company 51
signals from body 46
social survival 41
somatic meditation 46
somatic voice training 70
sounds, physical realization of 84
speech training 109
spoon story 51–52
standard operating procedures 16–18
student-centered self-assessment model 21
student(s): behavior or shares the personality that caused teacher to tighten 98–102; exceptional 104–108; midterm assessment 99; need 60–65; star 104–108
student talking time (STT) 9
syllabi with resources 14

talent 54
teacher-centered classroom 9

Teacher Certification Program 61
teachers: assumptions about students 54; harmful things 54; helpful things 53; understanding 54
Teacher's Nightmare, The 65
teacher talking time (TTT) 9–10
teaching evolutions 27–28
theater: importance of 3–4; teaching days 4; transformative power 4; value of 4
theatrical classroom exploration 68
theatrical speech training 86
think-pair-share 10
touch 70

ungrading 21, 23–24

vibration 70, 92, 106, 118
vocal ahimsa 44
voice class 16, 33, 70, 81, 99, 104–108

Walker, Pete 41
Wangh, Stephen 48
wanting muscles 45–46
Way of the World, The (Congreve) 51
white dialect coach for black stories 83–90
whole-body learning 31
whole-body yeses 45

yoga studio 63

Zoom 27, 71, 88, 91, 101